D0849528

THE MAXXIS GLOBAL FAMILY

THE MAXXIS GLOBAL FAMILY

ACHIEVING LONG-TERM VALUE FOR THE GREATER GOOD

by **Dr. Wally Y. H. Chen**

Marshall Cavendish
Business

© 2013 Wally Y.H. Chen

Reprinted 2014

Published by Marshall Cavendish Business
An imprint of Marshall Cavendish International
1 New Industrial Road, Singapore 536196

All rights reserved

No part of this publication may be reproduced, stored in a retrieval system or transmitted, in any form or by any means, electronic, mechanical, photocopying, recording or otherwise, without the prior permission of the copyright owner. Requests for permission should be addressed to the Publisher, Marshall Cavendish International (Asia) Private Limited, 1 New Industrial Road, Singapore 536196. Tel: (65) 6213 9300, Fax: (65) 6285 4871. E-mail: genrefsales@sg.marshallcavendish.com. Website: www.marshallcavendish.com/genref

The publisher makes no representation or warranties with respect to the contents of this book, and specifically disclaims any implied warranties or merchantability or fitness for any particular purpose, and shall in no event be liable for any loss of profit or any other commercial damage, including but not limited to special, incidental, consequential, or other damages.

Other Marshall Cavendish Offices
Marshall Cavendish Corporation. 99 White Plains Road, Tarrytown NY 10591-9001, USA • Marshall Cavendish International (Thailand) Co Ltd. 253 Asoke, 12th Floor, Sukhumvit 21 Road, Klongtoey Nua, Wattana, Bangkok 10110, Thailand • Marshall Cavendish (Malaysia) Sdn Bhd, Times Subang, Lot 46, Subang Hi-Tech Industrial Park, Batu Tiga, 40000 Shah Alam, Selangor Darul Ehsan, Malaysia.

Marshall Cavendish is a trademark of Times Publishing Limited

National Library Board, Singapore Cataloguing-in-Publication Data
Chen, Wally Y. H.
The Maxxis global family : achieving long-term value for the greater good / by Dr. Wally Y.H. Chen. – Singapore : Marshall Cavendish Business, [2013]
pages cm

ISBN : 978-981-4408-04-2 (cased)

1. Success in business. 2. Conduct of life. I. Title.

HF5386
650.1 – dc23   OCN851410209

Printed by Everbest Printing Co. Ltd

DEDICATION

For my wife, Ming-I, the top contributor to this book.
I am forever indebted to her. Her selfless support and
encouragement have helped me persevere on this long journey
throughout my career and life. Without her, I would not have
been able to bring this book to a successful completion.

And for all the Maxxis family members who helped construct
the world stage on which we can perform together.
I am humbled by our accomplishments and deeply proud
of each and every one of you.

CONTENTS

ACKNOWLEDGEMENTS

I AM TRULY GRATEFUL to the many people who offered their invaluable assistance in the researching, writing and editing of this book.

My most heartfelt appreciation goes to chairman Mr. Luo Jye for providing me the stage to perform and to put what I have learned into practice. Mr. Luo, being a man of discipline, sets a noble example for future generations to follow.

Many thanks go to Ms. Shin Yi Tan, who suggested that I share my story with Maxxis and encouraged me to write this book. Blessed with both wisdom and beauty, Ms. Shin Yi graduated from Emory University and brought her innovation and insight to Maxxis' marketing efforts in Asia, where she is instrumental to our branding strategies. Also, special thanks to Ms. Christine Chong of Marshall Cavendish and Ms. G.K. Khor.

For all of his assistance with this book and for our long-term friendship that began when we established our U.S. operation, I thank Mr. James Tzen.

For the wonderful memories and sustained friendship over the years, I am grateful to Chairman Lin Hsi Tong of Honor Well Mold,

Chairman Tan Yang Nam of Kian Hon Tyre and Chairman Wu Shiu Sheng of Chun Yen Testing Machine.

To Professor Stephen Chih-Yang Lu of the University of Southern California, I owe a debt of gratitude for his insightful input and his assistance with the structure of the Maxxis Triple 3 concept. And to Sharon, wife of Professor Lu, many thanks for offering a lot of valuable advice on this book.

My thanks go to National Yunlin University of Science and Technology for awarding me an honorary doctorate and for providing first-rate continuing education courses and other programmes for industry personnel.

Acknowledgement is given to Professor Po-Young Chu for sharing his in-depth knowledge of strategic planning. His advice was invaluable.

My sincerest appreciation is offered to Lenny H.K. Lee and Leonardo C.Y. Liao for their continuous devotion to ensuring Maxxis' development in emerging markets. And, again, thanks go to Mr. Lee for his tireless effort in coordinating the many aspects necessary to complete this book.

For their dedication of managerial and technical expertise, my genuine thanks to Tony Huang and David Tseng, who are two of our most experienced vice-presidents at Maxxis Taiwan. And, for their contribution and useful suggestions, much appreciation to Derek McMartin, Kellie Carter, Barbara Parsons, Jim Lentini, Mark Schaubroeck, Matt Clark and Susan Flowers. Ms. Flowers, especially, dedicated a considerable amount of time to this project.

To our global distributors, KCT (Saudi Arabia), Feng Shen (Nigeria), Nasco (Egypt), Datis (Iran), Tyremax (Australia), Swan International (Bangladesh), North Trend Marketing (Philippines),

PT. Atria Prima (Indonesia), Daytonasport (Malaysia) and all other loyal global partners, I humbly offer my thanks for their dedication to sales growth and helping build the Maxxis brand.

To our raw material suppliers ExxonMobil, Evonik, CSRC and Formosa Taffeta, I am very appreciative of their continuous technical co-development and support, and for the sharing of managerial experiences.

I offer my thanks to First Bank, Bangkok Bank and Bank of America for their assistance during our rapid expansion. Special thanks to First Bank for the co-sponsorship of the Maxxis Tennis Cup.

In addition, I would like to express my deepest appreciation to all of the other employees, suppliers, distributors and stakeholders who make up the Maxxis family. The countless examples of dedication, enthusiasm and integrity they have provided over the years inspired me in the writing of this book and continue to inspire me every day.

THE
MAXXIS
FAMILY

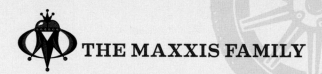

THE MAXXIS FAMILY

> To put the world in order, we must first put the nation in order; to put the nation in order, we must put the family in order; to put the family in order, we must cultivate our personal life; and to cultivate our personal life, we must first set our hearts right.
> — Kung Fu-tzu (Confucius)
>
> 明德于天下者;先治其國; 欲治其國者, 先齊其家;
> 欲齊其家者, 先修其身; 預修其身者, 先正其心 (孔子)

THE CHINESE BELIEVE that everything begins with the family. This belief stems from the teachings of Confucius, who also taught us to be tolerant of others and to be respectful towards them.

In *The Analects*, which is the collection of ideas attributed to Confucius, he said, "To put the world in order, we must first put the nation in order; to put the nation in order, we must put the family in order; to put the family in order, we must cultivate our personal life; and to cultivate our personal life, we must first set our hearts right."

These are beliefs with which I agree completely. Furthermore, as a Buddhist myself, I try to uphold these principles:

存好心
说好话
做好事

(*Have a good heart. Say good things. Do good deeds.*)

In my business practices, I apply these principles routinely and naturally. I believe that we must look after people and be responsible for what we do. If we make mistakes, we must be held accountable.

I'm in the business of making tyres. Because I care for my customers as people, I ensure that my company produces tyres that are of top quality. If they are not, accidents could result and cause people to lose their lives. I admit that this is also for my company's own security and the maintenance of its business, for if we continually produce tyres that are defective, who would want to buy them in the long run? But my highest priority is the safety of my customers.

Dr Wally Chen: We ensure that our tyres are of a high quality because our highest priority is the safety of our customers.

When I took over as president of Cheng Shin Rubber Industry Co. Ltd. in 1992, the company was already doing very well. In 1974, only seven years after its inception in 1967, it had become the biggest exporter of rubber products in Taiwan. From initially manufacturing bicycle and motorcycle tyres and tubes, it expanded its range to include these products in, among others, the passenger, truck and bus, and industrial and agricultural vehicle categories.

I carried on the company's legacy and introduced management values that aligned with my own beliefs. These are values that the company's employees have also come to uphold in their day-to-day work.

We now have an internationally recognised brand in Maxxis. This recognition came about because we felt it was important to create a brand that would be associated with high-quality tyres and be marketed globally. We export to 170 countries, which is phenomenal for a Taiwan company. We need to diversify our risks, so we sell to many markets. We are also constantly looking for new markets to increase our revenue margin. In order to compete with the giants in the tyre industry, we constantly employ new strategies. We are flexible, and we adjust to new trends. We act fast. I think our competitive edge is our sense of urgency, which has its roots in the fact that Taiwan doesn't have natural resources. Companies which begin in Taiwan must not only work hard, but quickly as well, bringing to bear the best efforts of their employees.

These are some of the factors that have propelled Maxxis International to ninth place in Tire Business' 2012 Global Tire Company Rankings, based on Maxxis' global sales of US$4.2 billion in 2011. Before this, we were in tenth place for several years.

I stress 100 per cent quality for the tyres we produce, and this is a message that our workers fully understand. I insist on 100 per

2012 Global Tire Company Rankings

Based on 2011 sales. Includes subsidiaries.

(Figures in millions of dollars, translated at average annual currency exchange rates)

2011 Rank	2010 Rank	Company/Headquarters	2011 Tire sales	2011 % of total corp. sales	2010 Tire sales	2010 % of total corp. sales	2009 Tire sales	2009 % of total corp. sales	2008 Tire sales	2008 % of total corp. sales
1	1	Bridgestone Corp.[1] Tokyo, Japan	*28,450.0	*75.0%	*24,425.0	*75.0%	*20,500.0	*74.0%	*23,435.0	*75.0%
2	2	Group Michelin[1] Clermont-Ferrand, France	*27,413.6	*95.0%	*22,515.0	*95.0%	*19,600.0	*95.0%	*22,820.0	*95.0%
3	3	Goodyear Tire & Rubber Co.[2,3] Akron, Ohio	*20,490.0	*90.0%	*16,950.0	*90.0%	15,649.0	96.0%	18,318.7[b]	94.0%
4	4	Continental A.G.[14] Hanover, Germany	*10,645.0	*25.1%	*8,100.0	*23.5%	*6,500.0	*23.3%	*8,100.0	*22.8%
5	5	Pirelli & C. S.p.A.[25] Milan, Italy	7,802.2	99.0%	6,320.5	98.4%	5,548.3	89.4%	6,003.2	88.2%
6	6	Sumitomo Rubber Industries Ltd.[12] Kobe, Japan	7,413.0	87.2%	5,850.0	85.0%	4,630.1	82.6%	4,843.9	82.9%
7	7	Yokohama Rubber Co. Ltd.[5] Tokyo, Japan	*6,028.0	*81.0%	4,750.4	79.2%	3,956.0	78.9%	3,976.6	77.3%
8	8	Hankook Tire Co. Ltd. Seoul, South Korea	5,744.2	97.8%	4,513.1	89.6%	3,760.0	93.5%	3,686.5	91.1%
9	10	**Maxxis International/Cheng Shin Rubber** Yuanlin, Taiwan	**4,268.0**	**100.0%**	**3,356.4**	**100.0%**				
10	9	Cooper Tire & Rubber Co. Findlay, Ohio	3,927.2	100.0%	3,361.0	100.0%	2,779.0	100.0%	2,881.8	100.0%
11	12	Kumho Tire Co. Inc. Seoul, South Korea	3,522.1	99.4%	3,025.9	99.8%	2,300.6	99.4%	2,593.3	99.2%
12	11	Hangzhou Zhongce Rubber Co. Ltd. Hangzhou, China	3,333.8	74.4%	3,226.1	97.2%	2,359.3	96.5%	2,126.4	99.8%
13	13	Toyo Tire & Rubber Co. Ltd.[6,7] Osaka, Japan	3,064.6	75.4%	2,500.0	73.6%	2,306.7	74.5%	2,410.0	73.7%
14	15	GITI Tire Pte. Ltd.[8] Singapore	2,893.6	100.0%	*2,207.5	100.0%	1,741.0	100.0%	1,931.3	100.0%
15	14	Triangle Group Co. Ltd. Shandong, China	*2,527.1	100.0%	*2,258.9	100.0%	*1,767.7	100.0%	1,767.2	100.0%

cent because it stands for the very best, a truism that even children understand. We want everyone — customers, employees, suppliers and others in our industry — to say, "If Maxxis is 100 per cent, how can you do better than that?"

We ensure quality control by printing a bar code on every tyre we make. With this code in place, we can trace who cured a tyre, who did the mixing, and so on. If a tyre is defective and causes an accident, we can find out who is at fault. I tell my workers that if they cause someone to be harmed in an accident, they are responsible. Their own friend or relative could be riding on these tyres, so our employees must be serious and focused in their work.

Our company exists because we want to provide value and service to our customers in the long term, so in tandem with quality, we must also provide value-creating, 100 per cent service. We need to come up with not only top-quality product design but also top-quality service design.

Service is a philosophy, and everyone in our company must internalise it in order to develop a service mentality. This holds true for everyone involved in the various processes of the tyre industry, from making the tyres to delivering them to customers.

I also stress the importance of giving and acquiring trust. When I took over as president, I decided I would be a leader through empowering others. Since then, I've given my trust to all my managers, at home and abroad. I trust them to take care of their own departments, their own regional offices, to make their own decisions. I may check periodically and ask about progress; otherwise, they have the authority to do as they see fit.

My goal is to create the greater good for every employee, to make everyone happy working with Cheng Shin/Maxxis. Everyone counts when it comes to building and growing a company. This of course includes our distributors. I tell them I'm not going after maximum profit; I'm more interested in optimal profit. I don't talk quarterly financial statements with them; I talk long-term sustainability and value. The profit must be sustainable because we have to grow, but everyone must have a fair share of the profit. I don't believe in a winner-takes-all scenario. People buy our tyres not only because of the brand and the quality, but also because of the work put into them by the people who sell these tyres. We think that 50 per cent is due to their promoting the product and providing the necessary service to customers, nurturing a positive, lifelong relationship. As such, the distributors deserve to get the rewards they have earned.

THE BRAND BELONGS TO YOU

I also trust our distributors, and I empower them. The Chinese have a saying: "If you are suspicious of someone, you should not involve him in your affairs. But if you want to, you must trust him." (用人不疑，疑人不用).

My practice is to let the frontline people almost completely control the business. Only the Taiwan, United States and Canada operations are fully owned by Cheng Shin. In Germany, we own only 20 per cent of Maxxis International. It's the same in Japan. In the United Kingdom, we have a 30 per cent share. I want the local people to own the company so that they will work harder.

In Africa, Asia, Latin America and the Middle East, we depend on our distributors, but even then, I let them take charge of the business in their own areas. I give exclusive distribution rights to only one distributor in each area. I don't have three or four, the way that some companies do. This is because these companies are driven by results, and they look at quarterly financial statements. As I've said, I look at the long term instead — the next generation. We work at getting the son to trust us like the father did.

In Malaysia, I always say Maxxis "belongs" to Kian Hon although they are only our distributor there. This motivates them to work harder. They take pride in the Maxxis brand and do their best to promote it. If the business increases, they also profit from it. And they know that as long as they conduct business and operate in the right way, I will never take away their exclusive distribution rights.

The growth of our relationship with Kian Hon, through trust and hard work, has resulted in much synergy between our two companies. In 2012, we collaborated on investing in the retread business, taking advantage of Kian Hon's experience in retreading and our ability to provide the rubber. At the same time, Kian Hon set up a training centre on its new premises so that we can share knowledge and the latest training with distributors throughout Asia and other parts of the world.

No Need to Talk Price

Even when I deal with our suppliers, I work to forge strategic partnerships. I don't haggle over price. I know that in return, our suppliers will reciprocate by providing us with technical support, software support and information about new products. For many people, profit is an absolute good, but I think that profit can be either good or bad. The bottom line is to look at the long term and work towards building lasting relationships. I believe that profit which comes at the expense of trust is bad by definition.

I have known David Wang for more than three decades, from when he was sales director at Monsanto, which provides chemical supplies to us. I used to tell him, "Regardless of the price, you just sell it to us." He told me years later how much he appreciated the trust I had given him.

I lost touch with him when he retired from Monsanto. But a few years after that, I received a gift watch from ABN AMRO and was impressed with it, so I asked one of my managers to find out who the supplier was. He told me it was a company called Rewen Co. Ltd. that supplied souvenir and gift items to businesses, and it belonged to David.

I asked to make an appointment with David, and our relationship was renewed. I then got him to supply our company with innovative gifts that we could present to our customers. He designed a special pen for us, something small enough to be put in a wallet. He was very pleased when I told him that our relationship falls into the category of "strategic partner".

"YOU GO UP 10 PER CENT, MY REVENUE DOUBLES."

Another of our strategic partners is Chun Yen Testing Machines Co. Ltd. We used to buy our testing machines from the United States, but the prices were high and the service was not what we wanted it to be. Then we discovered that Chun Yen's machines were just as good and the service was better. But I told them that we wanted machines done according to our design and they should not sell these machines to other companies, especially tyre companies. If they didn't agree, I would not do business with them.

They agreed. They knew that if our business was good and we expanded, they would also benefit. We have since been asking them to design new machines for specific uses. Now they have six plants in Taiwan, and three of them serve our needs. Half of their business comes from us.

Wu Shui Sheng, the owner of Chun Yen, said to me, "If Cheng Shin goes bust, we will also go bust. But before we entered the deal with you, we did research on Cheng Shin's other suppliers. We found that none of those companies had gone bust; in fact, they had actually prospered. So we were prepared to take the deal that required us to sell those machines exclusively to Cheng Shin. When we started, we were anxious, of course. But every year since then, Cheng Shin's revenue has gone up by double digits. When I supply to high-tech companies, their revenue curve goes up and down. But Cheng Shin's curve is always going up. If you go up by just 10 per cent, my revenue doubles. Even in the worst of times, your growth reached 16 per cent."

Chun Yen became a strategic partner because they had trust in us right from the start. We consider them part of our family. They help us in other ways too. For instance, we were looking to buy land in an area where we wanted to set up business. They knew of a plot that was available and even brokered the deal, and it turned out well for all of us.

THE PILLARS OF MAXXIS: QUALITY, SERVICE AND TRUST

Several years ago, I formulated a philosophy — the Maxxis Triple 3 system — to articulate what we are about, what we hope to achieve and what we should practise in our daily operations. Quality, service and trust are its pillars.

The underlying principles of Triple 3 guide us not only in our business and our work, but also in the way we conduct ourselves as human beings. The values we abide by at our headquarters are the same as those at our regional offices. This philosophy is also translated to our distributors, who are expected to do business with that same regard for values. And because Triple 3 is put into practice by our employees and distributors every day, all around the world, our customers respect and trust us. Trust and respect are essential if we are to keep our existing customers, and equally essential when we seek new ones.

Triple 3 is shared with everyone who is related to our business. And because I like to think of everyone related to our business as part of our family, I have placed right at the centre of Triple 3 something that I call the Maxxis family.

Confucius said, "The strength of a nation derives from the integrity of the home." It's the same with a business organisation. A business organisation is in a sense a large household, which means it may be considered a much-extended family. In the case of Cheng Shin/ Maxxis, the family includes not only the employees at our headquarters in Taiwan and the regional offices in other parts of the word; it also includes our distributors, our suppliers, our strategic partners and certainly our customers and communities. We are all part of a whole entity, so we look after one another. If any family members need our help, we do our very best to help them.

The Maxxis Triple 3 system is the foundation of our company's philosophy and practices.

Maxxis to the Rescue

For example, some years ago, a young student newly arrived in the United Kingdom from Taiwan felt hungry around midnight and went to buy something to eat at a 7-Eleven store. Unfortunately, he was mugged. Physically hurt and unsure of what to do, the boy called his mother in Taiwan. She couldn't help him there and then, but she remembered her friend who worked at Cheng Shin Rubber, also known as Maxxis International Co., Ltd., which had branches and subsidiaries in various parts of the world. She hoped her friend might know if there was a Maxxis in the U.K. Her friend, our international sales director Warren Lin, called the person in charge of Cheng Shin's export department in Taipei, who then called Peter McMartin, co-owner of Maxxis International UK.

As soon as Peter learned that this boy was in trouble, he was ready to help. He took the boy to the hospital to attend to his injuries and then to make a police report. He also went to the trouble of explaining to the principal of the boy's school what had happened. It was all settled very quickly. If it had not been for Peter's willingness to help, the boy's father would have had to go to the U.K. himself to see to the matter, but he wouldn't have been able to get there right away. In addition to the unavoidably long flight from Taiwan to London, he would have had to wait days for approval of his U.K. visa application. Both the boy and his family would have had to go through considerable anxiety. And because Peter's response was both prompt and compassionate, this young man received a level of assistance that would otherwise have been impossible — even had he worked through his own government's official channels.

Extraordinary occurrences like this provide vivid examples of the Maxxis family experience, but in reality, this sense of family can be found in even our most routine work, day in and day out. This sense of togetherness and belonging is ingrained among our employees and colleagues, and our actions to help each other, in ways large and small, spring naturally from that fact.

THERE'S SUCH A THING AS A FREE LUNCH

In most high-tech companies in Taipei, employees have to pay for their lunch. Cheng Shin is different. We offer free lunch in our cafeteria every working day to all employees, so that they can eat together and get to know one another better. There is nutritious food on the menu, with rice, noodles, buns, pork, chicken, fish, vegetables, soup, dessert and tea available every day. And we mark special occasions: If someone is celebrating a birthday, that employee will have a special dish to commemorate it.

This arrangement of ours has been around for a long time, since before I joined the company in 1974. It's just one of the things we do to make our employees happy and show them that they're valued.

When I don't have lunch appointments outside, I eat in the company cafeteria together with my managers. I eat the same food they do. After we've finished eating, they can approach me if they have anything to discuss. Sometimes, if there is a pressing issue involving several departments, we'll have an ad hoc meeting with the department heads then and there, allowing matters to be resolved quickly and the managers to have easy access to me.

Above all, we all eat together like family members. This is something valued by Chinese families; we are just maintaining the tradition.

I show respect to my staff. I don't shout when something goes wrong or when someone makes a mistake. I may tell whoever made the mistake that they are not doing a good job so that they are aware of the need to do better, but, unlike a lot of Chinese bosses, I don't shout at them. That's not my style.

American Relatives

The family concept is also built into the way we operate in the U.S. James Tzen, president of Maxxis International USA, makes sure this concept is imparted to the staff members there, and he shows it through his interaction with them.

When our employees in the U.S. fly to Asia, they fly business class, as James does. When he travels within the U.S., James flies economy like every other employee.

We have to treat our employees well, as though they are family. This respectful, generous treatment builds trust, and makes it more likely that the relationship will last. If you're part of a happy family, you'll work hard, and you'll be willing to make sacrifices. As an employee, you will exude the same spirit and attitude when you deal with customers, giving your customers reason to trust you. And in our experience, they will.

We compensate our employees fairly when they do a good job. And we do other things to instil that family spirit. James takes his staff for outings such as baseball games, and the company organises pot luck parties. They also come together to take part in community service events, like campaigns to donate books to charity or hand out canned food to the poor. During Thanksgiving, everyone gets a gift card worth a small amount of money, and each employee gets the same amount. At Christmas, they get presents. And to show that no one is favoured, James has them draw their own present. This practice also helps to cultivate a family feeling among them.

That is why Matt Clark, James' marketing manager who joined Maxxis USA in 2008, thinks our company is different: "Business culture can be harsh, and in the U.S., few companies put families first. But I think of Maxxis as a family. Maybe it's because I played a lot of team sports growing up, so any strategy I come up with is focused on what's best for our entire team, the whole Maxxis family. I know that if I ever have a problem that isn't work-related, I can bring it to James or Human Resources, and they'll be flexible and understanding. It's something that a family offers. I don't just think of collecting my pay cheque. I want to see the Maxxis family grow and prosper."

Hulen King, who is responsible for sales of bicycle, ATV (all-terrain vehicle) and motorcycle tyres for North America, appreciates the fact that we pay 100 per cent of our U.S. employees' health insurance, because he knows that employees in most other companies have to contribute a portion from their salary. He believes that Maxxis is concerned for the well-being of all its employees, as evidenced by our strong retirement benefits programme, in which the company matches a significant portion of our employees' contribution. "The company's retirement plan is top-notch and extremely generous compared to other companies in the U.S.," he said.

Hulen likes working for Maxxis because it is "team-oriented". Whether he's working with R&D or with his sales colleagues, all actions are taken as a team. He has seen how we allow our employees to make mistakes, try new things and push the envelope, because we stress the need to be innovative. So whether we are making tubular tyres for bicycles or trying something else that can revolutionise the industry, we're always seeking the best way forward.

Andy Lee, our sales director for automotive tyres in the U.S., says he likes working at Maxxis because we emphasise integrity. When he first joined the company in 1991, he was told that whenever he dealt with customers or prospects, he had to be fair and honest, because Maxxis looked for long-term business partners, not one-shots. He appreciates the fact that the company recognises people who work hard. Andy put his natural inclination towards hard work together with his business acumen, and less than two years after he joined us, he was assigned an overseas trip. It meant a lot to him, not only because it was his first trip out of Taiwan and few employees then got opportunities to travel overseas, but also because he was accompanying the R&D section manager and me, the president. For a junior employee, it was rewarding to work with seniors and observe them at close range in order to learn more about the business.

When our connecting flight in Bangkok got delayed, we were told we had to stay overnight there. But the airline gave us only one room to accommodate three people. It was of course unacceptable. I let Andy handle the situation although I knew his proficiency in English then was rather low; I wanted him to get the experience of finding a solution. To his credit, he managed to get us an extra room. I think he felt good about being the problem-solver for senior management in this situation, and he's been finding solutions for us ever since.

You've Got a Friend

A few years ago, at a management meeting in our Yuanlin headquarters in Taiwan, I told everyone present, "Remember, customers may pay for our products, but they buy because of their relationship with us." Andy was there, and he took what I said to heart. In his dealings with his customers, he works at nurturing these relationships and even tries to bring them to a higher level.

He told me of a customer in the U.S. he deals with now who was the first to give Maxxis USA business with his purchase of car tyres more than 25 years ago. James was handling him then, but even now that Andy has taken over, the customer still asks about James and Grace Ju, the lady who helped out with accounts when we started our U.S. office, every time Andy visits him. The customer had developed a relationship with James and Grace that was special; it was partly business and also partly friendship.

The customer would also ask about Lenny H.K. Lee, our global sales and marketing director, because he remembers how hard Lenny worked when he went to his warehouse many years ago to inspect tyres that consumers had returned over quality issues. Lenny, who was an engineer with the company then, spent virtually the whole day going through every single tyre and came up with a report listing the legitimate complaints and those that weren't. The customer agreed with Lenny's assessment and was very happy with his service. That's why he still asks after Lenny.

Lenny is one of the many employees who has a strong feeling of belonging regarding the Maxxis family. He has been with the company since 1989, and he still works just as hard as he did on his first day. His preoccupation with sales and marketing now takes him to Asia-Pacific countries, Australia, New Zealand, the Middle East and Africa. He's travelling every month, sometimes a few times a month, but he's still enthusiastic about his work.

There are many others like him who have been with the company a long time and have no desire to move anywhere else, because Cheng Shin is their home and they dedicate themselves to it — people like vice-president for culture building and branding Tony Huang, R&D Centre vice-president David Tseng, director of domestic sales Leonard Liao, director of R&D Department (Compounds) Ho Chin Fang, and senior production manager Lai Kuo Ti, who is in charge of our bicycle factory in Changhua County, Chung Chuang.

This factory is our biggest in Taiwan, and Lai manages it like clockwork. In order to meet requirements for production output, he makes sure that no time is wasted on the factory floor. This factory used to produce 110,000 bicycle tyres a day, but now it concentrates on only high-end products, mainly for export to Europe, producing 30,000 tyres a day. This factory uses our bar code system, ensuring that the right materials are processed in the right production line. If the barcode for a tyre is not the right one for a particular line, the machine will not process it. After processing, Lai makes sure that every tyre is checked at every stage of production. The signboard at his factory, as in all our other factories, reads: "Maxxis customers expect zero defects."

REAL ROLE MODEL

Then there is Chang Liang Hwai, our oldest staff member, who is in his early eighties and still puts in a decent day's work. Born in 1932, he is a real role model, a living example of 100 per cent loyalty. He feels a true sense of ownership towards the company. Cheng Shin is truly a family business for him, because his son and grandson work in our factory. Representing three generations, all of these employees have complete trust in Cheng Shin.

Chang was a curing worker who rose to become production manager. When he retired, I decided to put him on contract and made him production consultant. It's not a formal job; he's like a housekeeper who keeps the house tidy. You won't find this in a lot of companies. I set no working hours for him. It's up to him when he wants to come to work. Nonetheless, he comes into our Yuanlin

Chang Liang Hwai (right) is an example of 100 per cent loyalty.

factory every working day at 6:30 in the morning and checks every machine to see if there are any problems with it. He comes early so that he can get feedback from the night shift workers before they get off work.

You don't need to give him instructions, which I appreciate in any employee. But he takes his work seriously as he goes about monitoring the quality of our tyres. If he comes across a problem or if he thinks something is not up to standard, he will take it upon himself to fix it. If someone does something wrong, he will point them in the right direction. He has been in tyre-making since the age of 18, and he knows exactly what to do, because he's seen what works and what doesn't. His vast experience is highly valued by his co-workers and our managers, who also respect him because he is such a hard worker. Chang helps to improve our production process with his knowledge, his dedication, and by his example.

THE LONG TERM

Our distributors are also our family members. We take good care of them whenever they come to visit our headquarters in Yuanlin, providing them with comfortable accommodation and taking them out for meals. As the Chinese say, "If you come from far away, you are my friend. I have to treat you nicely."

Even when they get into trouble that is not caused by their own doing, we help them out. For example, in 2010, a big fire broke out in the free trade zone of Colon, Panama. Because of low water pressure, the firefighters could not completely put out the fire, and it burned for a few days. More than 20 big warehouses were completely destroyed, including the one owned by our Maxxis distributor for Panama.

All the tyres in the warehouse, close to 100,000 units, according to the inventory, went up in smoke. This caused a shortage in the supply of tyres in the market. The distributor was understandably anxious. So Paul Huang, Maxxis' sales director in charge of Latin America, met with me and a few others in our factory in Asia to urgently review our production status and assess what we should do in this emergency situation. We realised that our unfortunate distributor had been badly affected by the disaster and we wanted to help him as much as we could. Although our production schedule was pretty tight, we made a quick decision to organise a supportive shipment plan to Panama to supply much-needed inventory there. In return for what we did, this distributor has since been showing a high degree of loyalty and working harder to bring in more sales.

We acted as we did in Panama because we believe in maintaining long-term relationships. Such actions are also, in my view, evidence of our high regard for family values. Family members care for each other and help each other when needed.

Trust, respect and integrity are also critical to any relationship, including interactions among company stakeholders. With those ideals in mind, I tell my staff not to bring guests or customers to disreputable places. If other companies do that, that's their concern. But we are a family-oriented business and we should not engage in unsavoury practices. I tell my staff who are stationed overseas that if they indulge in such activities, I will transfer them back to headquarters. I don't want to destroy their families.

Of course, this means that I myself must set a good example. I must be a role model. I must lead a clean life and look after my wife and family. I do more than that. I look after the employees of my company, and certainly distributors and regular suppliers as well. They are family. Partners or teams can go separate ways once a project is over. But I say that being a family means that we should always be together. Our business DNA is similar. We are willing to sacrifice for one another, and for the family.

And if we have a happy family, as we do in Cheng Shin/Maxxis, family members will be more than willing to work hard and have the right attitude. It's really not a profound idea. It's actually quite basic.

FROM A BICYCLE TYRE SHOP...

FROM A BICYCLE TYRE SHOP...

> Success depends upon previous preparation, and without such preparation there is sure to be failure.
>
> — Kung Fu-tzu
>
> 有備則無患 (孔子)

CHENG SHIN RUBBER INDUSTRY CO. LTD. was founded in 1967 by my father-in-law, Luo Jye, a remarkable man. I admire him very much because he came from humble beginnings. When he was young, he sold sweetmeal for a living before becoming an apprentice to a tyre-maker. He had little money, but he had the desire to set up something for himself and a vision for achieving success.

Before he set up Cheng Shin, when he was starting out in the tyre business, he had a small operation in a small shop selling recycled tyres. He had no money then to buy fresh rubber, so he bought used tyres, buffed away the treads from the casings and then cured them. After curing, he carved the treads onto the tyres to create what might now be called "recap" tyres.

As time went on, his business grew. He got into partnership with his friend to set up a company called Lien Shin. When they eventually split up, Luo Jye formed Cheng Shin Rubber Industry Co. Ltd., which started by producing bicycle tyres and inner tubes as well as motorcycle tyres. The company gradually expanded to producing industrial, passenger vehicle and truck tyres, always moving forward technology-wise.

...To the Ninth Largest in the World

In 1967, Cheng Shin had an initial capital investment of about US$200,000 and a staff of 178. Now, it is the ninth largest tyre company in the world, the top tyre-maker in China and Taiwan, and it produces tyres in all categories, including automobile, light truck, motorcycle, ATV, bicycle, race kart, trailer, truck and bus, and lawn and garden. It sells to more than 170 countries, delivering high-quality tyres to both original equipment (OE) and aftermarket customers, and has more than 25,000 employees. Its revenue in 2012 was over US$4.5 billion. It has operations in Taiwan, China, Thailand, Vietnam, the United States, Canada, the United Kingdom, Germany, Holland, Japan and Dubai.

Japan was the first country to which Cheng Shin exported — way back in 1969, when the company formed a technical partnership with Kyowa Ltd. of Japan to manufacture bicycle tyres and inner tubes.

Then Luo Jye envisioned expanding the business further by aiming to export to the U.S. The company applied to the U.S. Department of Transportation (DOT) for recognition of its product quality, and in 1971, it obtained a DOT number, opening the door for export to the U.S.

To handle its rising export business, Cheng Shin built a new factory, dedicated mainly to producing tyres for export. It was ready by 1972, and in 1977, Cheng Shin opened a sales office in Taipei to handle the export trade.

THE U.K. CONNECTION

Meanwhile, in the U.K., Cheng Shin maintained its relationship with Peter McMartin, who had a business based in Felixstowe, Suffolk. He had known Luo Jye even before Cheng Shin came into being. In the early 1960s, Peter came to Taiwan seeking a source for motorcycle parts, and he found Lien Shin. After that, he started importing motorcycle tyres as well. As time went on, Peter expanded his business to include tyres for other kinds of vehicles.

When Cheng Shin was set up, Peter maintained his relationship with Luo Jye. This relationship has continued to the present, with Peter's son, Derek, in charge. Their company's name was formerly Bickers Anglia (Accessories) Ltd. Later on, it became a PLC (public limited company) with Maxxis serving under it as a division. When Maxxis International UK, also a PLC, was eventually set up, the situation was reversed, with Bickers becoming a division of Maxxis instead. Cheng Shin has a 30 per cent stake in the company. Thus, Maxxis UK is a subsidiary of ours, not a distributor.

Derek, a qualified engineer, has been with his father's company since 1996. He took over as managing director in 2003. Since then, he has been driving up sales to give Maxxis UK a higher market share penetration than Maxxis distributors in other parts of Europe. This has been possible because he works at instilling brand awareness among his main target group — tyre dealers. He adds value to our tyres by giving support to the brand through helping dealers with marketing and through sponsoring sporting events and getting endorsements from motor racers.

He has also been impressing upon dealers and consumers the quality of our tyres. He tells them our tyres require minimal balancing and less time to fit, and they agree. He hired an independent quality assurance consultancy in the U.K. to assess our quality. They came to our factories in Shanghai to test our tyres, and we were all pleased that they concluded that our products were better than those of some bigger companies.

U.S., HERE WE COME

I joined Cheng Shin in 1974 and was assigned to the planning department. I had had no prior knowledge of tyre manufacturing; my field of study at National Taiwan University was economics. After graduating, I wanted to go on to graduate school. I took the entrance examination and passed. But then, I decided that I would first perform my military service. After that, I felt that I didn't have what it takes to do further studies.

So I looked for a job and was hired by Cathay Pacific, where I was posted to the lost-and-found department. I found the job boring and left after three months for a job in the export department of a down jacket manufacturing company. Not long after that, I joined Cheng Shin, where I learned a lot in my first few years in the planning department, before I was entrusted with overseeing the export sales department.

James Tzen came to us in 1976 and joined the export sales department, where he worked closely with me for five years, before going to the U.S. to continue his studies. After he finished his studies there, we asked him if he would consider taking charge of our office in the U.S. if we decided to set one up there. In 1984, I went to the U.S. with him to check out the possibilities. People were suggesting that we locate the office in Memphis or Philadelphia, but I decided on Suwanee near Atlanta, Georgia, because Atlanta was then a growing city and a good distribution point. It is now the primary transportation hub of the American southeast. And the 1996 Olympics came to be held there.

In 1985, our U.S. office started operations with a staff of two — James and Grace Ju, who took care of the accounts. We sold bicycle tyres, then ATV and motorcycle tyres.

Grace is another person whose career provides a vivid example of the loyalty of many Cheng Shin employees. Instrumental to the building of our U.S. operation, she was employed by the company from its founding in Taiwan until her retirement in the U.S., a span of more than four decades.

A base of operations in the U.S. gave us the foundation to launch Maxxis as a brand and to take it further afield after that. In terms of branding and product development, it is still the best place to be. We used the U.S. as a testing ground for our brand. It is where you want to place your product because you get exposure there that you can't get anywhere else. If you can get consumers in the U.S. to develop a need for your product, chances are it will also create a need among consumers in other parts of the world. By the same token, if you are a known brand in the U.S., it's much easier for you to become known elsewhere, too. Furthermore, there are a lot of events and activities there that you can sponsor. And your sponsorship can reap benefits because of its prominence in the media — not only in the U.S., but outside as well.

If you sponsor a well-known baseball team, your brand will be seen in Asia and Latin America, places where there is a huge following for baseball because the games will be telecast there. It's the same with sponsoring a top-tier basketball team. Baseball and basketball are very popular in Taiwan, so it suits us well to sponsor the U.S. teams. Our customers in Taiwan can catch the games from the U.S. live and spot our signage when it comes on.

Today, our U.S. operations are already quite established. We have a warehouse located beside the office and a Maxxis Technology Center across the road. The Tech Center, as we call it within the company, was established in 1999 and is dedicated to R&D. An hour's drive away is an assembly operation that assembles ATV tyres for companies such as Yamaha. We have another warehouse in Texas, in a city called Grapevine near Dallas, and one in Rancho Cucamonga in California.

NEW MILESTONES

Before we started our office in the U.S. in 1985, Cheng Shin achieved a few new milestones at home.

In 1981, we built a new plant in Changhua County to produce high-quality bicycle tyres. At the time, Toyo, one of Japan's leading tyre producers, was looking for a partner in Taiwan because its competitors, Bridgestone and Yokohama, already had such partners. So Toyo approached Cheng Shin. In 1982, we signed a technical cooperation contract with Toyo Rubber Industrial Co. to build a modern radial tyre plant. This was a major boost for us.

In 1983, our total domestic and export sales reached US$90.4 million, vastly exceeding our expectations. We were ranked first within Taiwan's rubber industry.

In 1987, we became a publicly listed company. And the following year, our capital increased to US$54.4 million, which was a phenomenal increase from our starting capital in 1967. Our new plant in Hsi-chou was completed, and it began manufacturing bicycle and industrial tyres. We formed a partnership with Kyowa Ltd. to establish Cheng Shin Tire (Japan) Ltd. In 1989, we set up Cheng Shin Rubber (Hong Kong).

GREAT LEAP FORWARD TO CHINA

Around this time, Luo Jye, who had been planning to expand to China, decided to go there for an inspection tour. He saw the opportunities in China not only because it was a huge market, but also because it was culturally similar to Taiwan in many respects. At the time, most businesses were locating in Shenzhen, but we decided to set up our plant in Xiamen. It was appropriate because the people there speak Hokkien, as we do. In fact, a good number of earlier immigrants to Taiwan had come from that area.

The Xiamen plant was Cheng Shin's first overseas. Today, there are five plants in operation there. In addition to other things, they produce more than 30,000 bicycle tyres every day.

Luo Jye's decision to go into China was brilliant. The timing was perfect. When he moved into China, the country was undergoing economic reform and opening up to foreign companies. China welcomed Taiwanese firms and offered preferential incentives. Cheng Shin tyres have since become a respected brand in China, and we are Number One there in the sale of bicycle and motorcycle tyres. Another major brand of ours that is selling well is Sakura. And in 2004, Cheng Shin and Sakura became the first Taiwanese-owned tyre brands to be recognised as well-known trademarks of China.

In 2009, despite the worldwide economic slowdown, our sales in China increased by 15 per cent. The following year, they exceeded US$1.6 billion. Our first plants in China have been joined by factories in Chongqing, Tianjin and Kunshan. For a while now, we have been established as the top tyre-maker in the Greater China market, which includes Taiwan as well as China and Hong Kong.

SALES AND CAPITAL SOAR

I was appointed president on August 1, 1992. By then, the company was already well established and flourishing, thanks to Luo Jye's vision. My challenge was to take things one step further.

We aggressively increased our production capacity for passenger radial tyres. We invested US$8.4 million in building a new warehouse with an automated storage and retrieval system (AS/RS). Our capital increased to US$106 million, and in just four years, we had managed to double the capital with which we began in 1988.

Our sales in 1992 exceeded US$200 million and, in due course, we were getting recognition for the quality of our products. We were awarded the ISO 9001 certificate in 1994, becoming the first manufacturer in Taiwan to achieve that. In the same year, Ford Motor Company presented us with its Q1 Quality Award, given to companies whose quality management systems are up to Ford's standard. Ford designated us a Tier 1 and preferred supplier.

In 1996, our capital increased even more — to US$185 million. Such capital injections normally constitute reinvestment from our profits; we hardly ever ask our shareholders to put in more money. That year, Japan's Toyo Tire & Rubber joined with us and acquired a 30 per cent capital interest in Cheng Shin-Toyo Tire & Rubber (China) Co. Ltd. Together, we set up a new tyre factory in Kunshan. Our joint venture lasted until 2009, when we ended it by mutual consent.

More quality awards started to come our way as we headed towards the new millennium and began a new century. One of these was the Global Award for Outstanding Enterprise, given to Maxxis by Forbes in 2002. We received this award ten years after we first used Maxxis as a brand for our tyres.

The Wonders of Thailand

In 2002, near the end of the Asian economic crisis, I went with Lenny Lee and Hung Yu Lin, our vice-president for purchasing, to Thailand to find a partner to mix rubber there for shipment to Taiwan and China. As Thailand produced the highest-grade natural rubber that we needed, we thought the lower cost incurred in purchasing it directly and mixing it there at lower labour charges would be an advantage to us. I had not thought then of starting a business in Thailand.

Then we were presented with the opportunity for a new venture, and we realised that the investment environment was very inviting. The conditions looked good and we were offered attractive incentives. As Thailand was recovering from the crisis then, property prices were relatively low. Better still, foreign investors were allowed to buy land. They could also have 100 per cent ownership of their business; there was no need to operate it as a joint venture with a local partner. These conditions greatly changed my perspective on investing in Thailand.

When we returned to Taiwan, I asked Lenny to do a feasibility study on starting an operation in Thailand as he was handling exports to the Thai market. He came back with a positive report. I considered the plus points and decided to go ahead.

Only a year after our visit to Thailand, on March 6, 2003, we were already conducting a Buddhist ground-breaking ceremony for our new plant in Pluakdaeng in Rayong Province, complete with monks chanting blessings and firecrackers. And a year after that, the

Ground-breaking ceremony for our first plant in Thailand, 2003.

factory was ready. It is not normal for a factory to be set up so quickly, but the speed at which we worked to get it up and going is testimony to our management style. We always stress a sense of urgency when we need to do something that will bring us benefits.

Thailand was to be our first factory in a non-Chinese speaking country. It was a new milestone for Maxxis. And as part of our global concept, it constituted a new experience.

We sent employees from Taiwan to take up positions in Thailand. It was partly to give them the experience of working in a different cultural environment and to expose them to our global approach to business. I think that's good for them. I believe that trying new things is good for everyone, including our employees. Our staff did so well in this new environment that after two or three years there, a few of them could speak the Thai language pretty proficiently.

Without our Thailand factory, we would not be doing so well in the ASEAN (Association of Southeast Asian Nations) countries today. If these countries were to import directly from Taiwan, they would have to pay a substantial import duty. But because Thailand is an ASEAN member, it does not, under the ASEAN Free Trade Area (AFTA) Agreement signed in 1992, have to pay any tariffs when exporting to the other member countries, so this is a great benefit to us. This advantage has helped us to greatly increase sales to the ASEAN nations. Apart from this, Thailand is a strategic location because, for one thing, labour there is competitive. And, geographically, it is well placed for easy and cost-effective shipment of our tyres to other parts of the world, especially the Middle East.

Furthermore, Thailand was — and still is — one of the top rubber-producing countries in the world. So it's easier getting our supply of materials. And it also helps that the tyre industry is already quite developed there. Another plus factor is that when our Middle East customers look at the tyres and see "Made in Thailand" stamped on them, they are pleased.

After the new plant had undergone trial manufacturing, it was all systems go. It produced passenger vehicle, light truck, and truck and bus radial (TBR) tyres that were shipped to the 170 countries with which we had dealings. For passenger car tyres, in our first stage of production, we came out with 6,000 units per day. Now this plant produces a few times that number daily. Because of its operational success, the Rayong factory was to become the blueprint for two new plants in China — in Chongqing and Xiamen — for which the ground-breaking began in 2010. Another plant was also planned for Douliu, Taiwan.

Meanwhile, our Cheng Shin-Petrel factory in Xiamen, which was completed at the same time as the one in Thailand, also started rolling out products. In its initial stage, it reached a daily output of 700 steel radial light truck tyres per day. Few companies would risk building new plants simultaneously because it's a big risk, considering the bulk of investment required, but we have been doing this regularly. Sometimes, you have to take risks in order to reap rewards. Our record shows that taking calculated risks has worked in our favour.

AMONG TAIWAN'S TOP BRANDS

The year 2003 was also significant for us because it was the first time Interbrand, one of the world's largest global branding consultancies which specialises in, among other things, brand valuation, published its list of Taiwan's top 20 global brands.

Interbrand draws up the list based on each brand's financial performance, role and strength, and net present value of future earnings attributable to the brand. The brands that qualify must have a presence on at least three continents and have broad coverage in emerging markets. Thirty per cent of their revenue must come from outside the home country, and no more than 50 per cent from any one continent.

In that maiden assessment, Maxxis was ranked fifth, with a brand value estimated at US$256 million. Since then, we have been in the list for ten consecutive years. In 2012, our brand value was estimated at US$331 million.

In 2005, we decided to spread our wings to Vietnam as well. Vietnam had joined ASEAN in 1995, so it was also a beneficiary of the AFTA Agreement. The other positive points were that its labour is competitive, it is the world's third largest producer of natural rubber, and it is a huge market for motorcycle tyres. So we started construction of a new factory in Dong Nai Province after a ground-

Ground-breaking ceremonies in Vietnam, 2005 (left) and for our second plant in Thailand, 2008.

breaking ceremony in September 2005. In August 2007, this plant, too, began regular production.

In 2008, we embarked on a second plant in Thailand. With that and the ones opening in Chongqing and Xiamen starting in 2010, we expanded our production capacity to meet demand, which was growing despite the recession brought about by the global financial crisis of 2007 to 2008.

AMONG THE TOP 10 IN THE WORLD

We were highly rated on the stock market. Morgan Stanley's Taiwan automotive industry analyst, Jeremy Chen, considered our 2009 financial results "very strong". He saw us as a potential threat to the giants of the tyre industry: "We highlight that Cheng Shin's full year 2009 operating margin (20 per cent) remained well ahead of its peers' (12 to 15 per cent), providing more evidence of the company's strong competitiveness and execution capability. Although we expect margins and profits to fall this year, due to rising material costs, we retain an overweight rating on Cheng Shin, as we continue to see the stock as one of the best players on China's booming auto market."

The year 2009 was also favourable because we made the list of top ten tyre manufacturers in the world for the first time. We took the tenth spot, up from 11th the year before. With a worldwide sales revenue of US$2.723 billion, we replaced Kumho Tire Co. Inc. of South Korea, and managed to leap over Japan's Toyo Tire and Rubber Co. Ltd. and GITI Tire Pte. Ltd. of Singapore.

Our advancement was due to our continuously increasing output capacity through expanding our plants in Taiwan, China, Vietnam and Thailand; actively promoting our brands; and enhancing OE (original equipment) production for car manufacturing companies, including Shanghai General Motors Co., Ford, Daimler-Chrysler, Shanghai Volkswagen, Geely Automobile and Japanese car-makers.

It was predicted then that we would move up at least one notch in a year or two. And sure enough, in 2011, we made it to the ninth position. Our worldwide sales had increased to US$4.268 billion. We changed places with Cooper Tire and Rubber Co. of the U.S. We managed this by tapping into emerging markets and setting up new operations offices in India, Brazil, Panama, Dubai and other places to increase sales.

With our plants in Taiwan, Thailand, Xiamen, Chongqing and Kunshan in full operation, we were able to produce a total of 170,000 car tyres per day, up by 70 per cent from 100,000 the year before. On the Taiwan Stock Exchange, although its main index dropped 8 per cent in 2011, Cheng Shin's share price went up 20 per cent.

That year, Toyota presented us with a Regional Contribution Award for the Asia/Pacific region in recognition of our strong support in service and delivery, our efforts in using the Toyota Production

With Fujio Cho, the chairman of Toyota Motor Corporation.

System and the fact that Maxxis had had no quality issues for five straight years, from 2006 to 2010. I went to Nagoya, Japan, to receive the award from Fujio Cho, the chairman of Toyota Motor Corporation. I felt very proud that we had lived up to our commitment to 100 per cent quality.

After that, Maxxis was honoured by *Forbes* magazine by being included in its 2012 list of Asia's Fab 50 companies. It arrived at what it called "the region's best of the best" by examining 1,295 publicly traded Asian companies with annual revenues or market capitalisation of US$3 billion or more. Companies were evaluated on revenue, earnings, return on capital, share-price movements and outlook. The magazine also noted that the companies on the list were those that had managed to "thrive amid decelerating growth in Asia and all but non-existent growth in their U.S. and European markets".

R&D Rev-up

Despite receiving all these accolades, we are still committed to our quest for innovation and improvement. We continue to make R&D a priority. In 2006, we opened two new R&D facilities. One is near Shanghai, China, at the Kunshan plant, with space for 200 engineers. It is equipped with state-of-the-art machinery designed for testing force, rolling resistance, high-speed uniformity, noise and vibration, contact pressure measurement and analysis, and 3-D measurement.

To bring ourselves to a level where we can challenge tyre-producing companies that are much bigger than we are, we bought for the Kunshan tech centre a Flat-Trac III which is said to be the only machine of its kind being used in China. In the world, there are fewer than ten machines of this kind, and three of them are apparently owned by Michelin. We also installed in Kunshan a rolling resistance tester that can test tyre uniformity up to 200 kilometres per hour. It is also said to be the only one of its kind being used in China.

The other new tech centre is the one in Suwanee, Georgia, next to our U.S. office. It replaced the smaller Maxxis tech centre we had in Norcross, Georgia. This new facility expanded our capabilities for testing and development even further, with state-of-the-art equipment and a top-flight staff.

These two were in addition to our existing R&D centres in Yuanlin, Xiamen and the Netherlands. The one in Yuanlin is where our headquarters is located. This was our very first tech centre. Here, we have designed, created and tested numerous award-winning tyres. The one in Xiamen is responsible for the research into and development of new materials and compounds. It is also responsible for all the new product developments for bias and radial tyres. And the one in the Netherlands takes care of product development for the

European market; adhering to the mandatory requirements there, it creates and tests products specifically designed to European standards.

PROVING HOW SERIOUS WE ARE

Integral to our concern for R&D is our investment in a new proving ground using sophisticated technology in Kunshan. Its opening in November 2012 was one of our highlights for that year. China's basketball star Yao Ming was present to grace the occasion.

Located adjacent to our manufacturing plant, it covers an area of 860,000 square metres within a 5.2-kilometre perimeter. Costing more than US$150 million and taking a few years to design and build, it is most likely the largest in China. It is also the first one of international standard in that country.

We have made it a comprehensive facility so we can test our tyres under optimal conditions in order to improve their performance. There is a three-lane, 4.5-kilometre high speed track designed to allow cars to go as fast as 230 kilometres per hour. There is a dry skidpad which has been designed to be as flat as possible so that the handling of tyres under aggressive driving can be accurately tested. Another skidpad comes with six different surfaces for testing under wet conditions and simulated snow and ice settings. With this skidpad, we can test the performance of our tyres on surfaces covered with water up to 10 millimetres deep.

We can also evaluate how good our tyres are at negotiating different curves and at different speeds, and how they perform when they are subject to braking under a variety of conditions, including in snow and ice. We have the only equipment in China for measuring braking friction coefficients of tyres on road surfaces. The proving ground is also equipped with a noise, vibration and harshness (NVH)

Opening ceremony of our new proving ground in Kunshan, China, 2012. Standing tall is China's basketball star Yao Ming.

test course. It has eight different road surface designs and across them are five different roughness designs. This allows us to test for the level of comfort our tyres provide under each road condition. On the whole, our proving ground has more testing abilities than any other facility in China. It is a showcase of our seriousness in challenging ourselves to further improve and take our company to a higher level.

We have come a long way since 1967, and for us the way forward is always upward. But all this would not be possible if we hadn't been building ourselves up over the years, if we had not had farsighted leadership and solid management principles. As Confucius said, "Success depends upon previous preparation, and without such preparation there is sure to be failure." Our previous preparation has indeed brought us success. Now, we must continue to prepare for future success.

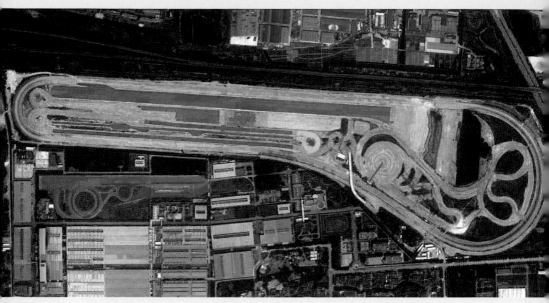

Aerial view of the Kunshan proving ground.

Cars testing Maxxis tyres at the opening ceremony.

The extent of the Kunshan proving ground.

With Yao Ming at the opening of our proving ground.

MAXXIS
IS THE
NAME

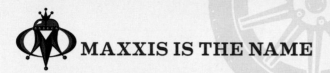# MAXXIS IS THE NAME

> The beginning of wisdom is to call things by their right names.
>
> — Kung Fu-tzu
>
> 必也，正名乎 (孔子)

IN THE LATE 1980s, I realised that if we were to go global, it was important to have a Western-sounding name for our products. If we didn't have one, we could be spending lots of money promoting Cheng Shin tyres, but the Cheng Shin name still wouldn't catch on, especially in the West. It's not easy to pronounce for those not familiar with Chinese names, and of course, it wouldn't mean anything to anyone who doesn't understand the Chinese language.

Another factor to consider was that if we continued to sell under the Cheng Shin name, we would probably have to keep our prices lower because people in Western countries tend to associate Oriental products with cheaper prices. With a Western-sounding name, we could sell quality tyres at double or triple the price. And of course, as a company, we would want to make better profits rather than sell at dirt-cheap prices.

Unlike today, when you have famous names such as the computer brands Acer and Asus, there weren't any famous brands in the West from Taiwan. Numerous Taiwanese companies that tried to make it in the U.S. failed and had to close down their operations there.

Our R&D was first-rate, and it is something we have always considered very important, but for me, that was not enough. I felt we needed branding, too. That was the way to ensure that we would grow. If we combined our solid R&D with a strong brand, I was sure we could take on the world.

I asked James Tzen, our Maxxis International USA president, to help with creating a new brand name. He got an advertising agency in the U.S. to come in on this, and we brainstormed together.

I had seven criteria for a good brand name: distinctiveness, brevity, appropriateness, easy spelling and pronunciation, likeability, extendibility and protectability.

The name is very important. It must be easy to remember and not be too long. Nike is easy to remember. So is Sony, which was previously known as Tokyo Telecommunications Engineering Corporation. The company used a shortened form of its Japanese name to refer to itself, but "Totsuko" was difficult for Americans to pronounce. Akio Morita, one of the co-owners, found that out when he visited the U.S. They tried using Tokyo Teletech, but an American company already had a brand called Teletech. Finally, they chose the name Sony, which is a composite of two words — *sonus*, the Latin root word for "sonic" and "sound", and "sonny", a term Americans in the 1950s used to refer to a boy. More than that, "sonny" had been adopted by the Japanese to form "sonny boy", which referred to young men who were smart.

It is said Morita and his partner, Masaru Ibuka, considered themselves "sonny boys", so the connotation rang true. So now everyone can remember Sony and say it easily.

We came up with a list of names and finally settled on Maxxis because it not only had a nice ring to it but also a few good connotations. It was derived from the word "maximum", which is a word with a positive meaning. When I think of Maxxis, I think of maximum power. It goes well with people riding bicycles or motorcycles using our tyres.

"X" in itself is a letter that exudes mystery. To young people, it sounds "cool". It goes with "Generation X", young and hip. It's the generation that is said to be open to diversity in society. To me, the brand name should appeal to the young because the Chinese have a proverb that goes, "When you are young, you have the potential to do whatever you want." (年輕就是本錢). We are constantly working to make friends with the young, from when they are small children riding bicycles, to when they are adolescents or young adults riding motorcycles to when they are working people driving cars. As they grow, we are always by their side. This is a lifelong association that benefits both them and us.

The double "X" gives the extra oomph to the word "Maxxis". I had learned this from ExxonMobil. When you pronounce the word, you can feel the emphasis provided by the double "X". It sounds forceful. It imparts the idea of toughness, which is one of the main characteristics of our tyres. They are built to last, and they are built to adapt to the terrain they traverse and the pressure exerted on them.

"M" is a letter associated with famous names like Mercedes, Microsoft and Madonna, so it sounded good to me. And the word "Maxxis" ending in an "s" sound recalls industry leaders like Philips, Siemens, Adidas, and even Rolls Royce.

As a whole, "Maxxis" worked. It had no negative interpretation in a different language, either. It could be used worldwide. So I was satisfied. We tested the name on a few tyres and found it was well-received. So we broadened the application to a wider range of tyres. We filed an application for the registration and use of the name in 1989. It was approved only in September 1992. That year, we started using it as a brand for our tyres.

Later on, an American company producing batteries wanted to name its product Maxxis, but we had already got the rights to it. They were willing to pay us a substantial amount for the rights, but we declined.

I'm glad we've stuck to the name. But branding is a long process. You have to keep spending money to promote your brand. You cannot expect to get returns in a short period of time. Because I tend to look at things in the long term, I could give a strong commitment to branding. One of the ways we do that is through sponsoring sporting events, vehicle races and competitions, and sports teams. We have been doing this for almost three decades now.

TEAMING UP WITH THE BEST

When we go into sponsorship in the U.S., the payoff is that many other countries will pick up on our brand quickly and easily. This is because many sporting events and competitions are telecast widely around the world. The games of the New York Yankees, for example, are watched avidly in South America and Asia.

The first big international sports marketing sponsorship we undertook was signing up with the Los Angeles Lakers in 1999. Since then, we have gone on to sponsor such U.S. teams as the New York Yankees, the Atlanta Braves, the Los Angeles Dodgers, the Chicago

Maxxis as official partner of the Baltimore Orioles. This photo was taken in July 2013 at Oriole Park, Camden Yards.

White Sox, the Detroit Tigers, the Washington Nationals, the Baltimore Orioles, the New York Knicks and the Houston Rockets.

We have also sponsored individuals. In 2004, we backed professional golfer Candie Kung during the LPGA (Ladies Professional Golf Association) tour season. She was born in Kaohsiung, Taiwan, and in 2003 she had won three LPGA events.

In 2005, we signed a multi-year endorsement deal with skating legend Michelle Kwan. She was a natural choice for us because we wanted only the best for our global branding efforts. She is the most decorated figure skater in U.S. history, having won five World Championships and eight consecutive and nine overall U.S. National Championships. On top of that, she has an Olympic silver medal won in 1998, and a bronze won in 2002. In 2003, she was honoured by the United States Olympic Committee (USOC) as Sportswoman of the Year. She has also been named USOC Athlete of the Month a phenomenal 14 times, more than any other athlete, male or female.

In my view, Michelle is a person of good character and therefore, a good role model. That was an important criterion in our choice of product endorser. In 2006, she was appointed public diplomacy ambassador by the U.S. State Department. She proved to be gracious and charming when she visited our Maxxis USA headquarters in Suwanee in April 2005. She still sends me a Christmas card every year.

Michelle Kwan during her visit to the Maxxis USA headquarters in 2005, with James Tzen (top photo) and Maxxis Automotive Territory Sales Manager Doug Addis.

Scoring with the Reds...

For me, the U.S. is the world's media and branding centre, and in order to build a brand, we need to start doing it in the U.S., then extend it to Europe and Asia and the rest of the world.

In Europe, where football is popular, we have been sponsoring teams like Liverpool, Sunderland, Tottenham Hotspurs, Everton and Aston Villa in the U.K., and Hamburger Sport-Verein in Germany.

Football is particularly appropriate for reaching out to tyre-fitters, a crucial target group for us. We figured we could instil awareness of our brand in them through the biggest-selling sport in their country since most of them would be interested in sports. If they could see our logo on their TV screens every week when they watched football, they might catch on that if we were branding at such a high level, our tyres must be worth checking out. And they could pass that on to their customers.

We started on a small scale, getting into English Premier League football with Aston Villa midway into the 2005/2006 season. It was partly to support our network of distributors by giving them the opportunity to watch some of the matches. The deal with Aston Villa made us an Official Partner of the club. We got extensive perimeter advertising at Villa Park, the team's home venue, and the display of large Maxxis banners around the field. We made sure our logo was visible at the corners of the perimeter so that whenever a team took a corner kick, TV cameras would pick it up. After Aston Villa, we moved from one club to another.

In 2009, we also sponsored a friendly match between the national England team and Trinidad & Tobago in the Caribbean.

Then in 2009, an opportunity arose for us to be an Official Partner of Liverpool Football Club, popularly known as the "Reds". At first,

Derek McMartin, the managing director of Maxxis International UK, discussed doing just banner advertising with Liverpool's director of business development, Jonathan Kane, but the club came back with the Official Partner offer. It was an offer too good to resist because

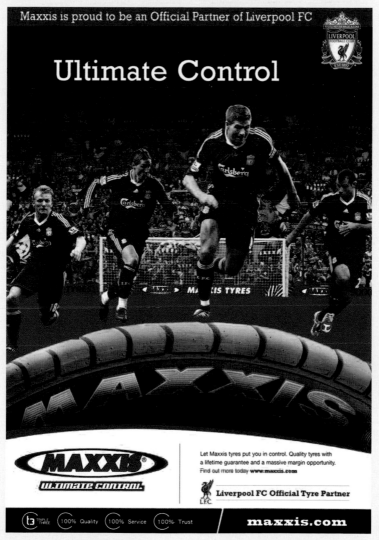

Maxxis as official partner of Liverpool Football Club.

Liverpool was — and is — one of the best-known football teams in the world with a gigantic fan base, and in terms of TV coverage, the deal would give us exposure to 6.2 million viewers in the U.K. and 2.6 billion worldwide.

This meant we got fantastic exposure for the local market, but globally, the Maxxis family could capitalise even more. For instance, we could give out posters of Liverpool to tyre shops in Germany, Spain, Thailand or Malaysia and they would put them up. This practice actually has a lot more effect than it would in the U.K.; a tyre shop in Birmingham or Southampton might not want the poster because it supports its own local club.

We have since extended our partnership through two three-year renewals, from 2010 to 2012 and from 2013 to 2015. As of 2012, Liverpool's global reach had gone up to 4.7 billion, which augurs well for us. Besides, we must have gotten off on the right foot, so to speak, with the club — just as our very first 20-second slot came on the LED screen perimeter during a match in April 2009, Liverpool striker Fernando Torres scored a goal. Press photographs that captured the image of the ball heading towards the goal caught Maxxis in the background. In slow-motion replay on TV, the Maxxis logo came across prominently. Few people could have missed it. What an auspicious way to make our advertising debut!

...AND WITH THE REST

In Norway, we focused on ice hockey and the team Frisk Tigers, which is one of the oldest ice hockey clubs in that country. It is also recognised as one of the best teams in Norway's ice hockey league, having won five league titles. We were with them from 2010 to 2012.

We are also an official sponsor of the Australian Open Tennis Championships, one of the world's four Grand Slam tournaments. This event attracts a lot of interest and coverage, so being associated with it enhances our brand value. In addition, Maxxis' corporate seating at this event provides an excellent space for entertaining our dealers.

Maxxis as official partner of the Australian Open Tennis Championships.

Chica Maxxis beauty contest in Ecuador, 2012.

Maxxis has also expanded its presence in Latin America in recent years, with great success. Starting in 2009, we set up two offices (Brazil and Panama), which collaborate with local distributors on many projects, including Chica Maxxis beauty contests which the company has held annually in several countries since 2010.

PAY LESS BUT GET FULL EFFECT

I'm particularly proud of our approach to sponsoring the Los Angeles Lakers. We were interested in sponsoring the Lakers because they were famous, and they were Number One, and we wanted to be associated with the top tier. By the time we signed on with them in 1999, they had already won about a dozen NBA (National Basketball Association) championship titles. This was an amazing record. The only team that had won more than the Lakers was the Boston Celtics.

Among the basketball legends who have played for the Lakers are Wilt Chamberlain, Kareem Abdul-Jabbar, Magic Johnson, Shaquille O'Neal and Kobe Bryant. The team holds the NBA record for the longest winning streak of 33 games. In fact, this long winning streak is unmatched by any team in any other professional American sport.

Sponsoring the Lakers wasn't going to be cheap, but I managed to work out getting a good deal from it without spending too much money. We entered the agreement with one-third of the season remaining. This meant that we spent only a little money to get maximum benefit. I had this idea from when I was a boy going to watch Chinese opera shows. If I went to the show late, I paid less money to the usher to get in. It was an arrangement that didn't hurt the theatre; in accounting terms, the seats that were not occupied were already part of the theatre's "sunk costs", so it made no difference even if latecomers didn't pay.

I applied this principle when sponsoring the Lakers. The rates offered were much lower because if there were no takers, the team would get nothing anyway. We got the sponsorship at only 20 per cent of what we would have had to pay for an entire season. But we got the same effect from it. We printed posters and distributed them. Those who didn't see the Lakers games could see our posters. They carried the Maxxis name, and it was as if we had been in there from the beginning. Our customers thought we paid a lot for the sponsorship; it gave them the impression that Maxxis must be a big company to be able to afford that kind of money. The deal was good for us.

I went to see one of the Lakers' games featuring Shaquille O'Neal and Kobe Bryant. That was an experience, but more than that, I requested beforehand that the management put on our Maxxis sign before the game started. Sponsor signs are rotated as the game progresses, so I thought if ours came on before the action started, it would get more visibility. After all, this was the time when the spectators would be waiting anxiously for the game to begin. They couldn't possibly miss our sign. And when they saw it, the sign would register more acutely in their minds. Besides, TV cameras would be able to pick up the sign more clearly since there would be no other action on court. But once the game started, everyone would be so engrossed in the playing that they wouldn't be bothered with whichever sign came on then.

I also didn't want our sign to appear at the end of the game because at that point, everyone would be more concerned with the score. They would not register the signs that came on then. And those watching the game at home would probably switch off their TV sets once the game was over, which would cut down the degree of exposure for the sponsor.

THE FIRST JOSS STICK GETS THE GODS' BLESSING

I think of all these things because I want to spend money wisely and effectively. When it came to sponsoring the New York Yankees, I asked for the Maxxis sign to come on in the first inning. It stays on for the first half of that inning until the next team comes up to bat.

I got this idea from observing what happens at a Chinese temple on Chinese New Year's Day. When the temple doors open, people rush in to try and be the first to put their joss sticks in the incense burner. They think the gods will give greater blessing to the people who are the first to worship them. By this token, my thinking is, when people see the Maxxis sign come on first, before other sponsors, they might have the impression that Maxxis is Number One. And this could motivate them to try out our tyres. I know we are not on the same level and our business is not of the same magnitude as, say, Toyota or AT&T, but we give consumers the perception that we are by appearing first in the Yankees' rotation of sponsors.

We started sponsoring the Yankees in 2003 and continue to do so, except for a gap in 2005. I thought it was good value for the money, because their games are telecast live in Taiwan and then repeated a few times afterwards. They are also seen in Japan and South Korea, and in Central and South America. So although we spend money in the U.S. to sponsor the Yankees, the visibility of our brand is high in Asian countries that follow baseball.

Our distributor in Vietnam watched a Yankees game one night, and when she saw the Maxxis sign appear, she cried. She had not expected to see it. She told me later that she had been in business with Maxxis for ten years and when she saw that sign, it made her feel proud.

TAIWANESE YANKEES AND ORIOLES

We decided to sponsor the Yankees because it is also a team in the top tier. Legends who have played for the Yankees include Babe Ruth, Lou Gehrig, Joe DiMaggio, Mickey Mantle and Yogi Berra. The Yankees hold MLB (Major League Baseball) records for having won 18 division titles and 27 World Series championships. This means no other team has won as many World Series championships. No wonder it constantly enjoys such great popularity; in 2011, the Yankees had the second-highest MLB attendance. These numbers are, of course, good for advertising exposure.

What also attracted us to the Yankees was the fact that it had a Taiwanese player. At the time we signed on, Wang Chien Ming was relatively new to the team. He was to make his mark a few years later when he was considered the Yankees' ace pitcher for the 2006 and 2007 seasons.

In 2002, Wang played for the Taiwan national team which won the silver medal at the Asian Games. He also represented the country at the 2004 Olympic Games in Athens. In the preliminary round, the top four teams qualified for the semi-finals, but Taiwan missed it by ending up in fifth place.

In Taiwan, Wang is considered a national hero. For a while, newspapers and TV stations in Taiwan were talking about him practically every day. Some commentators were even saying that if he ran for the presidency of Taiwan, he would win.

I went to watch Wang play some months after we took on the sponsorship. It was the first time I had stepped into the huge Yankee Stadium in New York City. There were about 45,000 people watching the game, and that wasn't even full capacity. The lowest-priced seats were placed way up high. It was amazing for me because in Taiwan, we don't get such a huge crowd at a baseball game, maybe about 2,000 people on average.

I had my son with me, together with James Tzen and our global sales and marketing director, Lenny H.K. Lee, who is based in Taiwan. My son was thrilled. We saw families gathered at the stands and children wearing Yankees T-shirts and eating burgers. They were in a celebratory mood. Watching the game was a whole-day outing for the entire family. That gave me a good feeling. We saw the signs of giant companies like Toyota, Ford and AT&T appear after ours.

James said to me, "It's good to be joining their ranks, isn't it? Especially for a company from Taiwan?" Lenny agreed wholeheartedly. I felt good about that, too.

New York Yankees pitcher Wang Chien Ming towering over me at Yankee Stadium.

Before the game started and after the players had warmed up, we got to meet briefly with Wang. This meeting had been prearranged by the management at our request, and we met in the bullpen area. He was very tall, about 6' 4". We gave him the pineapple cakes that Taiwan is famous for and took pictures with him. He signed the Yankees T-shirts and baseballs we had bought from the stadium shop. I remember he couldn't shake hands with us because being a right-handed pitcher, he couldn't risk hurting his pitching arm, otherwise known as his "Taiwan Golden Arm". I could understand that; his arm must be worth millions. Even in March 2013, after returning to the Yankees on a Minor League contract — after having suffered injuries continually and after going off to play for the Washington Nationals for a few seasons — he could be worth, according to his agents, up to US$2.5 million a year, plus US$2.2 million in bonuses.

The tie-in with Asian markets continues to influence our sponsorship decisions. In 2012, we signed a deal with the Baltimore Orioles because of the Taiwan connection in the form of its starting pitcher, Chen Wei Yin.

Chen is the Orioles' first Taiwan-born player, so to us, that was doubly significant. Before joining them, he spent some years with the Nippon Professional Baseball (NPB) league, playing for the Chunichi Dragons. He also played for the Taiwan national baseball team in the 2004 and 2008 Olympic Games.

After he joined the Orioles, he made his debut in Major League Baseball against the New York Yankees. The game was played 12 days after we had signed to be a sponsor of the Orioles. We saw the game live in Taiwan, but the Orioles lost in extra innings. For the rest of the 2012 season, however, the left-handed Chen was considered "the only constant in the Orioles rotation", and his performance was consistent.

CATCHING LINSANITY

Another Taiwan connection was forged when we sponsored the New York Knicks for the shortened 2011–2012 season, with Jeremy Lin becoming an almost overnight sensation there. Within ten days of being called upon as a starting player for the team, he scored so many points that the term "Linsanity" became a part of the basketball vocabulary. This surge in popularity led to his being featured on the covers of numerous sports magazines and other publications.

The following season, when we heard he had joined the Houston Rockets, our Maxxis USA marketing manager, Matt Clark, immediately called the firm which handles our advertising placements with sports teams. It seems they had been waiting for Matt's call. They had anticipated that we would see the global marketing opportunity in sponsoring the Rockets because of Lin, as he would be watched closely in Asia as well.

The deal was made and we became an official partner of the Rockets. For that, we get courtside LED signage exposure and four club-level tickets to every home game. We send the tickets to our Texas office to give away to our distributors as a sign of appreciation. We are also mentioned during half-time at every home game when the Rockets announce whom they will be playing in their next away game. They call this the "Rockets on the Road" in-arena feature, and at the end, they say that the feature was presented by Maxxis.

We always try to get the maximum value out of our sponsorship. For example, on December 14, 2012, the Rockets gave us a night to promote ourselves at their game against the Boston Celtics. We chose to produce 15,000 posters to give away, on a first-come, first-served basis, to the people coming into the stadium to watch the game; we put the posters in Maxxis bags to further promote the Maxxis name. With the Yankees, we secured the rights to print T-shirts with the Maxxis and Yankees logos on them for restricted, non-commercial distribution. Earlier, in 2000, we decided to sponsor the Atlanta Braves baseball team, partly to allow our customers to watch their games. We saw this as a good way to let them know that they are part of the Maxxis family.

Maxxis as official partner of the Houston Rockets; (opposite) the
Maxxis brand name in lights at the Toyota Center in Houston, Texas.

We were attending a tyre exhibition in Las Vegas when we heard that the Rockets would be in Atlanta to play against the Atlanta Hawks. We got James to contact the Rockets to say we were coming for the game and they arranged VIP tickets for us. On November 2, 2012, I went with a few friends and colleagues to watch Lin play. Among the Maxxis USA colleagues with me were James Tzen, human resources director Kellie Carter and business affairs manager James Chou. From Taiwan, there was Lenny.

We drove early to Philips Arena. It was the Hawks' first home game of the season and they were favoured to win, so there was almost a sell-out crowd. We were told the attendance at the game was 18,238 and the capacity of the Philips Arena is 18,750. The atmosphere was electrifying. While I had felt something like this at the Yankee Stadium several years ago, this was more intense because the space in this indoor stadium was more intimate. Once the game started, I was so engrossed in it that I became oblivious to the people who were accompanying me.

As it turned out, the Rockets won the game, by 109 to 102. I was very pleased to have been present to witness their victory against the odds. Lin played about 40 minutes and nearly scored a triple-double, with 21 points, 10 rebounds and 7 assists. I felt proud watching this athlete of Taiwanese descent shine in front of so many people. What made it even more poignant for me was that Lin's family hailed from the county of Changhua, where the headquarters of Cheng Shin/ Maxxis is located. His parents emigrated to the U.S. in the mid-1970s and Lin was born in Los Angeles, but as far as I was concerned, he was still one of us.

Right after the game, the Hawks representative took us to the area where Hawks fans wait to meet their favourite players. Then the head of security for the Rockets came and escorted us to a private room to wait for Lin while he was winding down from the game.

After waiting for quite a while, we got all excited when the door opened, but it wasn't Lin coming in. Instead, it was Harry the Hawk, the home team's mascot. We tried to hide our disappointment by posing for pictures with him.

A few minutes after he had left, the door opened again. This time, it was the Rockets' head of security coming to inform us that Lin was almost ready. He apologised for the long wait and explained that Lin had to appear at the post-game press conference first. This raised our expectations, and we started discussing which area of the room we should take pictures with him in.

Just as Lenny was in the midst of rearranging a few pieces of furniture to give us more space to move around, and some of us were noisily making alternative suggestions, Lin walked in. Everyone was speechless. He was wearing a long-sleeved round-neck T-shirt with "Houston Basketball" printed on it.

Kellie then took the initiative to introduce every one of us to him. She told Lin that Maxxis was the official sponsor of the Shanghai Maxxis Sharks, a team in the CBA (Chinese Basketball Association), of which Yao Ming is the owner. Lin, of course, knew Yao because the latter played for the Rockets from 2002 until his retirement in 2011. By the way, Yao was Maxxis' endorser in Asia from 2009 to 2012.

Lin was very friendly and took the time to shake everyone's hand, and also to pose for individual and group photographs. I presented him with pineapple cakes and Maxxis Coffee made in Malaysia. Compared to the Yankees' Wang, Lin seemed more open and extroverted. He smiled a lot. He appeared rather pleased that we were from the same

county as his parents. All in all, we spent less than five minutes with Lin because he had to leave to catch a flight back to Houston. But before he left, he signed three Rockets jerseys for us.

Overall, everyone had a lot of fun at the game and meeting Jeremy Lin. It was definitely a special treat for all of us and one that we will never forget.

Jeremy Lin with James Chou and Kellie Carter.

Jeremy Lin and me.

REFINING AND EXTENDING THE REACH
OF THE BRAND

As I've said, we must continue to improve in all aspects of our business, and branding/marketing is no exception. Frequently working together, our U.S. and U.K. marketing operations have been leading the way in refining and extending the reach of our brand.

Customers associate Maxxis with a certain look, so the right logo is crucial. With this in mind, our marketing team has recently begun to bring an old logo of ours back into use. This classic Maxxis logo provides more space for our company name and thus greater visual impact than the current well-known symbol. As the logo is simple, it can be more easily used in a consistent way around the world, thus strengthening our brand identity. It is also in line with current trends, as many well-known global brands have turned to a minimalist logo design. We're gradually introducing this classic logo, with the long-term goal of having it used uniformly around the world.

Facebook and other social media have had a seismic impact on marketing over the last several years. Our U.S. office has been aggressive in this area, appointing Megan Salo as our U.S. social media coordinator. Megan's work has been stellar, resulting in an enhanced Facebook presence and increased interest from Maxxis fans. She and her co-workers use social media to maximum effect to promote Maxxis products, sponsor drivers and teams, and to build the brand.

Our U.K. operation is working on a new website with enhanced capabilities, making a site visitor's experience more enjoyable and productive. In addition to many other improvements, this new site will include a map feature that enables visitors to find an official Maxxis centre in their country of interest. The new Maxxis.com will also be much more interactive, allowing for additional product information and high-quality images and videos. Maxxis' U.S. and Latin American operations will adopt the new website, thus strengthening brand identity by offering a more consistent message and look.

I am happy that our brand promise of 100% Quality, 100% Service and 100% Trust is being delivered to the public by a top-flight marketing operation.

THE BRAND BELONGS TO EVERYONE

THE BRAND BELONGS TO EVERYONE

> Make happy those who are near, and those who are far will come.
>
> — Kung Fu-tzu
>
> 近者悅，遠者來 (孔子)

DUE TO THE EXTENSIVE BRANDING we have done, Maxxis is no longer thought of as a Taiwanese company in most parts of the world. Sometimes, it is even automatically considered an American company. Derek McMartin, the managing director of Maxxis International UK, tells us that consumers in the U.K. think Maxxis is American. This proves the importance of having the right name.

When I thought of the idea of such a brand name in the late 1980s, it was a practical necessity because Taiwan was at the time not noted for producing quality products. In reality, that was not always true. Unfortunately, however, perception is the name of the game. You may say that your product is good because it really is, but the moment you tell the foreign customer, who doesn't know better, that you are from Taiwan, she will straight away think the product is not good. Or, at the very least, not good enough. And if she forms that opinion, she probably will not buy what you produce. In the unlikely event that she does buy your product, her purchase will only be possible at a greatly reduced price.

We wanted to grow, and in order to do that, we had to go global. We could go to China and sell Cheng Shin tyres without any problems, but outside of the Chinese-speaking regions, we had to use Maxxis. I'm glad to note that after all these years, Maxxis has lasted and provided us immense growth. Nowadays, U.S. buyers know we are a company from Taiwan, but they have come to accept that we produce quality tyres.

Sometimes, you have to assume a different guise to convince people of what you can do before they will accept you. But once you have proven your abilities, it won't matter to them anymore where you originated.

Nike, a company famously successful around the world, is an excellent example. While the company is American, its products are manufactured in Asia. Because of Nike's strong brand and international appeal, however, consumers display a preference for its products without regard to where they are produced.

In 2012, the Maxxis brand was ranked by Interbrand, the global branding consultancy, at number nine among the top 20 Taiwan global brands, with an estimated brand value of US$331 million. In evaluating the brands, Interbrand uses a financial analysis which measures overall return to the company's investors, the percentage of purchases which can be attributed to the brand, and the ability of the brand to create loyalty, demand and profit. Interbrand said Maxxis was "perceived to be the tyre brand with the highest cost-benefit ratio".

Among the other factors cited were our strong production output despite the global recession and the rising cost of raw materials.

This is a significant achievement for us. We are proud that in a little more than 20 years since we started the Maxxis brand, we have come this far. For ten years in a row, we have been in the top ten, and we are the only tyre company on the Interbrand list.

We spend about two per cent of our yearly revenue on brand building. This roughly amounts to US$67 million, an amount that is equivalent to the full-year gross profit of some technology giants. But I think more than just money is responsible for our success in branding; we have made solid progress because we have followed some important principles of brand building. Here are ten of them.

PRINCIPLES OF BRAND BUILDING
BEHIND MAXXIS' SUCCESS

First, we have kept our focus and done the right thing in choosing whom and what we sponsor, how much to spend and how to get the best return. This is the same laser-sharp focus we bring to our business. We realise that the tyre business is a highly competitive one; we are competing against every manufacturer from everywhere for everything. I always tell my staff and distributors this so that they can respond accordingly. Above all, anything we do is for the purpose of enhancing the brand, not merely selling tyres. This is a case of deciding to put the horse in front of the cart rather than the reverse. You can sell a certain number of tyres without brand building, but if your brand is strong and well-known, you'll sell many more.

On top of developing our tyres and other products, we also have been developing secondary product brands, like our Maxxis Grass Jelly and Maxxis White Coffee. We market them to our dealers so that when they have customers dropping by to have their car tyres changed or for some other service, they can serve the customers these products. A cup of Maxxis White Coffee could help the customer feel more welcome. He could feel he's getting personal service on top of the service he's getting for his car. It's part and parcel of the package we advocate — the dealer builds a relationship with his customer while the latter becomes more aware of the Maxxis brand. These strengthened relationships add value to the brand. Our colleagues, suppliers and distributors also think this is a fun approach to enhancing brand awareness which can, in turn, promote sales.

Second, we have cultivated a passion for winning. In sponsorships, we associate ourselves with industry leaders, and in the sports arena, we back teams that are winners, like the New York Yankees and Liverpool. In tennis, we don't simply sponsor any championships, but a Grand Slam, like the Australian Open. These things matter. They also give us the best exposure we can get. And customers associate us with winners.

In that spirit, we tell our distributors that even in bad times, we can make profits. In my annual letter to them in 2013, I said that as we faced a worldwide financial crisis, rising unemployment, higher material costs because of the scarcity of natural resources, and even more ferocious competition, we needed to commit all the more to making Maxxis the Number One choice of consumers.

Third, we commit ourselves to sustaining our brand because we recognise that it is a never-ending challenge. I am constantly reminding all Maxxis family members of the need to maintain our quality and service so that we can retain the trust of our customers. I also encourage them to be ambassadors for our brands. On our part, we show by example the importance of providing service.

Whenever we invite our distributors to a meeting, for instance, we make sure we pick them up from wherever they are, or from the airport if they are flying in from somewhere, and take them to the meeting venue. We provide for their comfort and see to their board and lodging if they are required to stay over. We treat them to sumptuous meals to welcome them and when it's time to say farewell, we ensure that they go back home safely. At every point of contact, we give them 100 per cent service. From this example, we hope they show the same to their customers. This is the same hospitality we extend when dealers come to visit us at our headquarters in Yuanlin; we spare no expense in making them feel welcome.

Fourth, we always consider the consumer the boss. The customer is a scarce asset. The quantity is fixed. You can buy machinery, you can buy materials, but you cannot buy customers. So how do we attract more customers and keep their business not just once or twice but for a lifetime? We believe in giving 100 per cent respect and 100 per cent care in our dealings with them, and in never taking advantage of them. We believe that conducting ourselves with integrity is central to building lifelong relationships, and it also instils brand loyalty. We try to befriend young children, from the time they start riding bicycles, and we continue when they move on to motorcycles. We hope that because of these early experiences, when they grow up and drive cars, they will choose Maxxis.

Fifth, we advocate that our work teams must be versatile enough to perform a variety of functions rather than merely specialise in what they are doing. This has worked very well for us thus far. We have engineers who started out designing our tyres who have moved on to marketing, and they have done so successfully. It makes sense for our staff members to learn other functions so that they can understand

Dr Wally Chen with our distributor in Saudi Arabia, April 2007.

the tyre business more thoroughly, and consequently be more knowledgeable and motivated to improve our brand of products.

We expect the same of our distributors. We encourage them to be self-managing and self-organising, and to be able to adapt to changing conditions quickly. In order to meet these standards, they must know the business thoroughly and commit to a common goal. They must be knowledgeable about what needs to be done to promote the Maxxis brand.

Sixth, we must constantly innovate, not just at headquarters but also in every region of the world where we do business. Under the Maxxis brand, we are always developing ways to improve our products. We set up advanced R&D facilities and state-of-the-art proving grounds. We invest in new plants. We constantly remind our distributors to come up with new ways to promote our brands and develop new strategies to sell our products. We tell them we often have to challenge the status quo and do things differently, and that we must be the ones to lead change.

Seventh, we believe that alliances create advantage, so we join up with companies like DuPont. I wanted to use Kevlar®, the tough synthetic material that it developed, for the inner lining of our bicycle tyres as protection against punctures. So I signed a deal with DuPont that lets us use it exclusively. We put a Kevlar® label on the sidewall of each tyre and that helps enhance our brand as well because DuPont is a big name.

Eighth, we must always act quickly. We believe that in business, larger companies will not necessarily win out over smaller ones; the quickest ones will instead reap the harvest. We therefore emphasise this principle to all our family members. In this ever-changing world, we need to have a sense of urgency and address what needs to be addressed as quickly as we can. Our factories have to bring out new products quickly to add value to our brand, our salespeople have to deliver them without delay, and our orders have to be met promptly. Without this sense of urgency and concomitant speed, we will not be able to live up to our commitment to 100 per cent service.

Ninth, we make our distributors our partners. In reality, all business is about people selling to people, whether the product being sold is an airplane or a washing machine. In applying that principle, we are one of only a few companies that deliberately choose local people to handle local business. We give 100 per cent trust to our distributors outside of Taiwan to handle their own local business. In that regard, they are truly our partners. We understand that they can conduct their own local business more effectively than we can because they are familiar with the local culture and they know the local language. They can build close relationships with their local customers and work towards gaining the highest share in their local market over the long term.

We usually don't take partial ownership of their company because we want them to derive maximum benefit from being their own boss. Neither do we exert any control over the local businesses. In this way, the Maxxis brand belongs to the local businesspeople as well. We believe in sharing profit with our distributors. This is the best way for them to take pride in what they are selling.

Tenth, we all have to work as a connected entity, with everyone recognising that they are a link in a chain, with every link maintaining its strength so that the chain remains strong. That chain is Maxxis. I learned from reading the book *The Connected Company* by Dave Gray of the strength inherent in a connected organisation. Such an organisation can adapt, move fast and respond quickly to customers who are also connected through access to new technologies.

A connected company can have a huge advantage over its competitors by seizing opportunities, while the latter are analysing risk. A connected company can rely on its network to tap into new possibilities and expand its influence. This is the new way forward, in contrast to the old way of companies working in isolation. This is why we don't exert control over our partners. We prefer a system that is dynamic and innovative, one that can adapt quickly and easily to the ever-changing marketplace.

A CULTURE-RICH BUSINESS

We believe in a culture-rich business rather than a cash-rich one. That's a big asset that's not shown in the balance sheets. The key to managing an organisation is establishing a good working culture. With a strong culture in place, the company can function without supervision. The employees know what to do and how. Similarly, with Maxxis, we strive to steep our distributors in that same culture so they also know what to do and how.

Integral to this culture is the brand. Maxxis' brand promise is 100% Quality, 100% Service and 100% Trust. This promise is something that everyone related to us knows and promotes. It is central to their existence as members of the Maxxis family, so to speak, like the air they breathe. The 100 per cent promise distinguishes us from others, and we are connected by this credo. When consumers see Maxxis, they think of the 100 per cent promise on quality, service and trust. That is our goal.

I also say to the local distributor, "The Maxxis brand belongs to you. When you sell it in your country, it also belongs to your country." I want each country to think this way when they see Maxxis, rather than identifying our company as a Taiwan brand. If they are Nigerian, I'd like them to see it as a Nigerian brand. If they are Guatemalan, I'd like them to see it as Guatemalan. They won't have to think that because it's not their national brand, they shouldn't buy it; they can make Maxxis their national brand in the 170 countries in which our products are sold!

Our "prosper thy dealer" approach has worked very well. That and our brand building efforts have resulted in numerous benefits. Our sales have been increasing every year. More people seem to be talking about Maxxis, and we've seen increased attention from the media as well. As the Chinese saying goes: "It is more blessed to give than to receive." (施比受更有福).

We get a lot of repeat business from customers who are loyal to our brand. We know this from the inquiries we get on our website, Maxxis.com. Many of the customers who visit our site are there to

Dr Wally Chen, fourth from right, with the distributor of Nigeria, Feng Shen, at Cheng Shin Group R&D Center building. Third from left is Daniel Wu and on the far right is Lenny Lee.

look for the nearest Maxxis store or for new products. We also know from the feedback we get that many customers ask for Maxxis when they replace their worn-out tyres at their regular service centres.

When we introduce a new product, it creates interest among potential buyers because our strong brand has acquired a good measure of credibility. The branding gives us a clear, valued and sustainable point of differentiation relative to the competition. We are able to sell at higher prices, which means we can give our distributors higher margins. Strong branding creates a win-win situation for them and us. On the whole, this translates into higher revenue and higher profits, which constitute better returns for our shareholders and stakeholders. We are able to reward our employees substantially and keep them satisfied. This is essential for attracting as well as retaining the best workers. We are also able to reinvest our profits to further improve our infrastructure and develop better products.

The brand is like an account. Every interaction with the consumer will give you either a positive result or a negative one. If it is positive, you add money to your account. If you don't treat your customers well, your account will be negative. The purpose of doing business is to be sustainable and competitive, and to gain advantage. A brand is forever. If you have a strong brand, it is your most valuable asset. Legal protections mean that your brand is your own and no one can take it from you without repercussions.

Make the Elevator Go Up

Despite the success we have achieved with our brand, we are not going to rest on our laurels. We are trying to further increase brand value. I have come up with a theory to explain the importance of enhancing product value and why branding is necessary. I call it the Maxxis Elevator Theory.

Clients served by a contract manufacturer will always ask for a lower price for the latter's product. This is the case particularly when the manufacturer engages in the OE business. If the price is too low, the manufacturer will obtain lower profits. And if the client keeps asking for even lower prices, the manufacturer may not be able to meet the requested price and the client will move to another manufacturer. This is a great disadvantage for contract manufacturers.

By way of example, let's look at an iconic American shoe brand. Because it's so well-known, this brand can sell a pair of sneakers for US$90 and make a margin of US$22.50. The contract manufacturer that supplies the shoes to this iconic brand, on the other hand, earns only US$1.12 per pair. Thus, the margin for the iconic brand is 20 times that of its supplier's.

Let's look at another example. Compare a branded T-shirt with an unbranded one. In terms of materials, they are basically the same, but the T-shirt that carries the logo of a well-known brand can usually be sold for a profit of up to ten times more than that of the unbranded one. The same situation prevails with wristwatches. Street vendors sell no-brand watches for as little as US$4 each, but there are consumers who will pay hundreds of thousands of dollars for luxury watches marketed by well-known brands.

These instances, which are part of everyday life all over the world, inspired the Maxxis Elevator Theory.

I use the elevator as a metaphor. We take an elevator to go up or go down. In the theory, UP signifies enhancing value and DOWN signifies lowering costs. If a company goes up by enhancing the value of its goods, the amount of increase can be infinite; the sky is the limit. On the other hand, if the company goes down by lowering costs, there is a limit to how much these costs can be reduced. This process is governed by economic principles: If lowering costs results in the company making a loss rather than a profit, it will be headed for collapse. Its elevator will plummet.

VALUE UP:
The sky's the
limit

COST DOWN:
An endless
downward spiral

The Maxxis Elevator Theory: The product's variable cost is the pricing floor. The limit is whatever the customer is willing to pay.

Enhancing value is obviously the better option, a result which can be achieved through branding. With a strong brand, a company can enter previously untapped markets and achieve greater profits. But if a company doesn't have a strong brand identity and equally viable distribution channels, it will be trapped in its concern over costs and what prices it can charge. Therefore, in a highly competitive market, a company can easily fall into a deadly spiral by focusing solely on price. Its elevator will just keep going down and down.

Slashing prices is therefore not a viable strategy. Enhancing product value is most certainly the way upwards.

THE MAXXIS CURVE

A concept called the Smiling Curve is frequently used to discuss the importance of branding and marketing. In a Smiling Curve graph, the vertical axis shows the degree of ROI (return on investment) while the horizontal axis represents the various stages of the life cycle of a product: R&D, manufacturing, branding and distribution. The degrees of value added on the extreme left and extreme right sides — for R&D and marketing — are much higher than that for manufacturing. The resulting curve resembles a smile.

When this concept was revealed to Taiwanese companies, most of which were contract manufacturers, they realised to their amazement that they should no longer put emphasis on manufacturing and economic activities that have low value added, but instead, focus more on R&D, branding and distribution. After a long period of study and observation, we came up with the Maxxis Curve, which reinforces the effects of the Maxxis Elevator Theory.

Although they may appear similar, there are important differences between the Smiling Curve and the Maxxis Curve. The Smiling Curve

Maxxis Curve

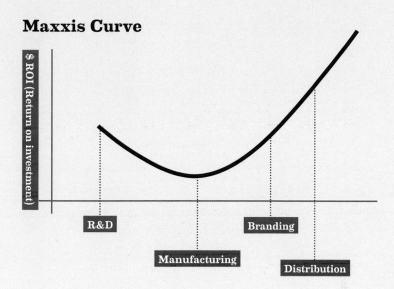

is symmetrical, while the Maxxis Curve is not. The Maxxis Curve is weighted towards the right, showing higher ROI on branding and distribution as opposed to R&D and manufacturing.

The emphasis on branding is important in order to establish Maxxis' reputation and brand image. Maxxis' distribution channels also come into play here, bringing the company worldwide exposure. This focus on branding and distribution results in a Maxxis curve which is shaped somewhat like a spoon rather than being perfectly symmetrical.

The reason for the higher values provided by branding and distribution lies in manufacturing's relatively higher cost. Integral to most manufacturing operations, assembly lines are the most labour-intensive portion of the supply chain. They require an outsized portion of a company's total labour force and consequently, the lion's share of total costs. Adding to the many strains on manufacturers is the fact that those costs are increasing throughout the world. These ever-increasing expenses are the reason that manufacturers frequently move their factories to countries with less expensive labour. Sometimes known as "nomads", these companies' profit margins are actually shrinking, in large part because they compete against everyone, from everywhere, for everything, all the time.

These facts and the results of our study have led us to invest our resources more heavily in branding and distribution. This allocation maximises the value of our resources and allows us to create brand value, thus allowing us to compete on terms other than cost.

Semi-conductor chip-maker Intel is a good example of a company that employs this strategy. If Intel had not seen the value of marketing and branding, they would have had no means of standing out from their competitors because their product is only one component of a larger whole. So Intel requested that computer brands using Intel chips insert an Intel image and the phrase "Intel Inside" in all their advertising. This branding ensures that Intel is easily recognised by end-users. Thus, as Intel built up its brand image, consumers began to develop a preference for computers with Intel chips. Today, Intel has the largest share of profits in its industry.

Adhering to the principles of the Maxxis Elevator Theory and the Maxxis Curve, we have made branding and marketing our priority.

Customers are Friends

To increase our sales channels and gain additional customers, we have been going into new countries such as Indonesia which has a huge market. This is in addition to the 170 countries where we are already selling. Apart from securing more OE business in order to link our tyres to well-known car brands, we are putting up more signboards

(left) Facade of a Maxxis store in Jeddah, Saudi Arabia; (right) interior of a Maxxis store in Dammam, Saudi Arabia.

and setting up more Maxxis stores and Maxxis service centres.

In Taiwan alone, we have about 160 Maxxis service centres and 700 Maxxis stores. In Europe, we hope to set up about two dozen of them in due course. We plan to set up Maxxis service centres in the Middle East, and the prototype for those centres has already been designed.

We have significant presence in Malaysia with 20 service centres. Kian Hon, our Malaysian distributor, has been putting up more billboards along the Malaysian North-South Expressway to create increased awareness among Malaysians. Kian Hon is also promoting our brand through social media. Kian Hon created a Maxxis 4×4 Club on Facebook, and in a matter of eight months, the page achieved 5,000 likes. The people who clicked "like" were not enticed by freebies or giveaways, which means they are sincere followers. And they are people from all over the world. Such is the wonder of social media, and we are determined to maximise our use of this highly effective marketing tool.

Maxxis service centres and Maxxis stores are enterprises run not by us but by independent owners. They can sell other brands as well, but they have to commit to selling a certain percentage of Maxxis tyres; for example, in Taiwan, the percentage is 70 per cent for Maxxis service centres and 40 per cent for Maxxis stores. They all carry the Maxxis signboard on their frontage.

We help the owners set up their stores and service centres, and give them special prices on our tyres. We ask that they follow the store design and decorations we have set for them. If we come out with a new product, we give them priority access to it. We also protect them by not having more than one store in the same area. They are required to sell Maxxis tyres as a priority and to promote our products, but they can also provide other services such as selling accessories and providing maintenance for cars. We impress upon them the importance of giving 100 per cent service to their customers because we are lending them the Maxxis name. As a result the owners treat their customers like friends, providing them with a place to rest while their tyres are being fixed, and serving them tea and snacks.

There is a shop called Kian Chiang Tyres in Yuanlin which started out on its own and switched to being a Maxxis service centre after six years. Since signing up with us, its business has been improving every year. The owner, Chuang Hsiu Ling, attributes the growth partly to the 100 per cent service her shop provides. She keeps a file for each of her customers so that she can update them when their tyres need servicing. When a customer celebrates a birthday, she texts him or her a greeting. If an area is hit by floods or a typhoon, she sends out messages to customers in that area to warn them to be careful.

She also tries to help when a customer experiences an unexpected problem. Once, when a customer's car broke down while she was on

(left) The Maxxis brand maximises exposure with roadside billboards and banners; (right) Maxxis motorcycle tyre distributor Daytonasport Sdn. Bhd. with local dealer at the product launch of Maxxis Volans in Malaysia, June 2013.

her way to eastern Taiwan, she called up Chuang for advice on what to do. Chuang then called a Maxxis store near where the car had broken down and an employee went to fix the customer's car.

Another reason for Kian Chiang Tyres' growth is the effort we put into marketing our brand. We sometimes help with sponsorship of local events, like a blood donation drive or a tennis tournament. This helps to attract new customers. We also advertise on TV, and Chuang told me there have been cases of customers sending her photos they had taken of the Maxxis logo when they saw it appear on TV. There is a sense of community in all of this which I find truly heartwarming.

Another example of a distributor going to extraordinary lengths to assist a customer occurred in the southern part of Thailand. One of our distributors there is an expert in feng shui (风水), the art of arranging one's surroundings in a way that maximises the positive energy of the space. When a customer confided his business problems to the distributor, the latter volunteered to visit the customer's home and office with an eye to providing advice on feng shui. The customer took our distributor's advice on rearranging his surroundings and when he called our distributor a few months later, things had completely turned around. His business had picked up and his problems had eased. His good fortune may be chalked up to coincidence, but he was grateful for our distributor's concern. This customer is now quite loyal to Maxxis and feels a personal bond with our distributor. There is a moral to this story: Every bit of assistance counts when it comes to customer service.

A similar example of unconventional customer service occurred in Bangkok. The wife of our distributor there holds a management position in Shiseido, the internationally known cosmetics company. When she arranged a cosmetics class for the wives of Maxxis' dealers, the response was uniformly positive and the class went a long way towards creating goodwill towards Maxxis. While make-up and tyres may seem completely unrelated, in our case access to one product helped us sell the other.

MORE
VROOM
TO THE
BRAND

# MORE VROOM TO THE BRAND

> There is no contention between gentlemen. The nearest to it is, perhaps, archery. In archery, they bow and make way for one another as they go up and on coming down they drink together. This is the way gentlemen contend.
>
> — Kung Fu-tzu
>
> 君子無所爭，必也射乎！揖讓而升，下而飲。
> 其爭也君子（孔子）

MAXXIS SPONSORS a lot of sporting events and tournaments because our products are for outdoor usage. Motor sports, in particular, are closest in terms of relevance, so we sponsor motocross and other racing events extensively. In fact, I could say without much fear of contradiction that there is a Maxxis-sponsored racing event going on somewhere in the world almost every day.

We place emphasis on sponsoring racing competitions in which our tyres can be used. These events give us international exposure and, more importantly, provide us with what are essentially portable laboratories, allowing us to continually test and improve our products — with the support of racers. Their performances and feedback help us to better evaluate the quality of our tyres.

Among the major racing events we sponsor are the Enduro World Championship; the NitrolympX in Hockenheimring, Germany, which is one of the biggest drag racing events in Europe; the Dutch Supermoto Championship in the Netherlands, in which many current and former world champion bikers take part; Night of the Jumps, in which the best daredevil riders attempt to outdo one another in performing the most amazing acrobatic stunts on their motorcycles; Bavaria City Racing in the Netherlands, in which all sorts of racing cars and bikes drive through the city centre of Rotterdam; the TKM Karting Festival at which only Maxxis tyres have been used since the go-kart racing competition started in 1989; the British Drift Championship; the Australian Motocross Championships; and many more in Thailand, Japan and China.

Australian Josh Walters strives for more pace in his Maxxis-sponsored Milwaukee Yamaha.

Maxxis Italian Quadcross Championship 2012.

And those contests are just a sample of our event sponsorships. You can see that we are involved in a wide range of competitions, involving a host of different vehicles and different forms of racing — from go-karts to ATVs, encompassing street racing, daredevil riding and desert rallies as well as those on conventional circuits.

SHORT COURSE OFF-ROAD RACING...

In the U.S., we sponsor short course off-road truck racing, which is said to be the fastest growing discipline in all motorsports and therefore excellent for providing exposure. Usually, our sponsorship gets us banners on the track, pit space for our support truck, decals on sponsored drivers' suits, and logos on drivers' suits and helmets. But we are also attracted by the national TV coverage for this sport.

In response to the growing popularity of this racing discipline, we have even built a special race tyre called the Razr SCR for the larger truck classes, Pro 2WD and Pro 4WD. In the smaller truck classes,

CJ Greaves' short course race truck, competing in Crandon, Wisconsin, September 2012.

drivers use the Maxxis Bighorn.

We sponsor many outstanding drivers in major short course off-road series. I'm proud of our relationship with Marty Hart, a champion with experience in several racing disciplines. Marty has won more than seven national championships and the Baja 1000, with titles in three-wheel, four-wheel and off-road racing vehicle categories.

"We've been out there for about seven or eight years, or maybe even longer, through rock crawling and the short course world," Marty says of his relationship with Maxxis. "Overall, you not only have great products but great people. That's something that Maxxis has over anybody I've ever worked with. From the engineers to Brad [Williams], to the guy who oversees the tyres at the races, you're not just a number. [At other companies], there was no depth of relationship, and it was just win or lose. I felt that I was a number. This is more of a personal relationship and personal development. I think that's huge. It just makes success easier when there's a lot of open communication.

You have to make split-second decisions in short course racing, and that's easier when there's a relationship with all parties. Everything you do is affected from the top down, whether it's a problem with a product, or on the other side when it's a win. Most companies only have a rep who goes to the track, and you only deal with that one guy. Maxxis isn't like that, and it's been a pleasant experience."

DESERT RACING...

Drivers sponsored by Maxxis have repeatedly put our products to the ultimate test in the gruelling SCORE Baja desert races. In a contest so difficult that just finishing is considered a significant accomplishment, many of the sport's best pros wouldn't consider using any other tyre.

ROCK CRAWLING...

Rock crawling also interests us. This sport is an extreme form of off-road driving involving drivers using vehicles ranging from stock to highly-modified, whose challenge is to overcome obstacles. The vehicles usually employed are four-wheel drives like trucks, jeeps and buggies. As the name suggests, the drivers compete over harsh terrain that has boulders, foothills, rock piles, mountain trails, etc. The more impassable the obstacles, the more challenging the experience for them.

We sponsor both W.E.ROCK (World Extreme Rock Crawling) and the Ultra 4 Series (King of the Hammers). These two exciting series feature different objectives. W.E.ROCK is a rock crawling series that has competitors complete a series of obstacles within a set time, rather than engage in head-to-head racing. Ultra 4 is head-to-head endurance racing that combines desert sections as well as rock climbing sections.

(top and middle rows) Maxxis SuperB Dakar Team, Lima, Peru, 2013;
(bottom left) Maxxis Philippines Cebu 4×4 competition, 2008; (bottom
right) Maxxis International USA support truck.

Maxxis AT-771 poster.

Short course driver Johnny Greaves with the Razr SCR tyre.

AND DRIFTING...

And then there is drifting. This is an exciting driving technique which causes a car to slide as it takes a corner at high speed by braking rear tyre traction and counter-steering the car out of the turn. The effect of this manoeuvre causes the car's tyres to smoke.

The sport originated in Japan, and Kunimitsu Takahashi is credited with being the creator of drifting techniques in the 1970s. One of the first drifting contests was held in Japan in 1986, and as the standards of drifting drivers rapidly rose, a race series developed around 2000, called D1 Grand Prix. Drivers are judged by entry speed, racing line, drift angle and the amount of tyre smoke, or, in other words, show factor.

The sport caught on in the U.S. in 2003 with the setting-up of Formula DRIFT. From there, it spread to the U.K. It has also become popular in Southeast Asia with the establishment of Formula

DRIFT Asia and in New Zealand with its NZ Drift Series. Drifting has developed into a legitimate motorsport worldwide with an ever-increasing fan base. That's easy to understand because it is a crowd-pleaser, and its freestyle nature has caused it to be compared with skateboarding. Unlike other motorsports, drifting allows spectators to see the entire race from their seats because most competitions are held at motorsport arenas. During the economic downturn of 2009 and 2010, it was one of only a few sports that experienced a growth in attendance.

In the U.S., Maxxis sponsors Formula DRIFT as an official supplier of tyres to the series. We supply the Victra MA-Z1 Drift, a tyre specifically designed for drifting, featuring a special tread compound that generates clouds of tyre smoke and offers excellent vehicle control beyond the traction limit.

We also sponsor drivers and teams that compete in Formula DRIFT because our involvement builds a performance image for our ultra-high performance tyre line-up. Sponsorship also gives us exposure

In the semi-finals of the 2013 Maxxis British Drift Championships, both Maxxis-sponsored teams, Japspeed and SATS Motorsport, competed against each other.

among the younger 18- to 39-year-old male demographic who follow the sport in arenas and on TV and the Internet through live streaming and on blogs. And because drifting is relatively new, it gives grassroots drivers a better chance to become professionals without having to win multiple feeder series and have the right business connections. This aligns well with our philosophy and practices because we are known as a grassroots company.

Ryan Tuerck is a drifter whom we sponsored for several years before he left to work with another company. He's since returned to Maxxis, and we're delighted that he's back on board. "Maxxis has been a huge positive factor in my career thus far," says Ryan. "Maxxis offers one of the best tyres on the market for my discipline, to be able to compete at the highest level in drifting. The staff behind Maxxis are also great; they're great people to work with. They have a very good understanding of and relationship within motorsports, which makes it a lot easier to relate to one another while trying to fulfil the common goal that we all have, which is winning."

Formula Drift racer Ryan Tuerck on the MA-Z1 Drift tyre.

We saw one of the people we nurtured, Chris Forsberg, come up through the ranks and work his way to becoming a champion. We signed him when he was just a grassroots racer on the east coast. After a few years, in 2009, he became Formula DRIFT champion. That year, he was also Tires.com Triple Crown Champion and Formula DRIFT Driver of the Year. Although he no longer drives with us, we're proud of what he accomplished as part of the Maxxis family.

While loyalty is rare in motorsports, as a brand, Maxxis has been able to attract racers willing to take less money in order to be part of what they consider a great family. On our part, we feel good that we now have top-notch racers wanting to be part of our team when not too long ago, we were considered almost a nobody in the world of racing sponsorship.

Motorsports do help create an aura for the brand, and we have had fans of Maxxis express their affinity for the brand in creative ways. One fan carved a pumpkin to make it look like a Maxxis tyre. Some have cut their hair to make it approximate Maxxis tread patterns. Some celebrated Earth Day by making belts out of old Maxxis bicycle tyres. And one especially devoted fan named his dog Maxxis. These enthusiasts are often opinion leaders within their social circles, so they act as influential brand ambassadors for us. It's a good approach — influence the influencers.

MOTORCYCLE AND ATV RACING

For cross country racing, there are two premier series — the GNCC on the East Coast and WORCS on the West Coast, both featuring professional and amateur dirt bike and ATV racing. Professional racers from these series have played an integral role in the development of

(left) Maxxis quad at Dakar Rally, January 2013; (right) Mike Penland.

our tyre lines. We have won numerous professional and amateur championships in both series, most notably through competitors like Bill Ballance, Chris Borich, Beau Baron and Mike Penland, one of the first riders we sponsored in the U.S.

Mike came on board with Maxxis in 1993 and has ridden our tyres ever since. A legend in the world of UTV (Utility ATV) racing, he's a six-time class winner of the gruelling Baja 1000 race and has won 11 GNCC class championships. He has assisted with our UTV product development and is one of the most popular draws to the Maxxis booth at industry trade shows, where he cheerfully meets with fans and signs autographs for hours at a time.

"I started with Maxxis in June of '93, and I feel they make superior products," Penland says. "They give me more than I could ask for. I feel that they make the best tyres you can buy as far as traction and durability. Maxxis has done everything they said they would do. If they say they'll jump straight up six feet, that's what they'll do — in fact, probably seven feet. And the Bighorn tyre, virtually every company there is copies it. If there was ever a tyre that I could put my name on, it would be the Bighorn. And they're good people — James [Tzen], Barbara [Parsons] and everyone I've ever dealt with there."

Within his sport, and among his many admirers, he's as well-known for being a truly nice guy as for his racing achievements. I'm proud that we have earned his loyalty over the years and equally proud to have him as a member of the Maxxis family.

Maxxis also supports the AMA ATV Motocross National Championship Series, which features the very best ATV riders along with top amateurs. The series offers categories for riders as young as four years old and for machines from 50cc to 450cc. Riders race on a small, closed course circuit featuring jumps, turns/berms, whoops and a start gate.

CYCLING TO GLORY

In cycling, we are an official partner of the exciting USA Pro Challenge, a seven-stage race that goes around the state of Colorado over stretches of mountainous territory. It was first held in 2011 and has become, in a very short time, one of the premier road cycling events in the U.S. It is estimated that over a million spectators come to the race. There is extensive TV coverage with broadcasts to 175 other countries and territories. At the sponsorship level, we get one kilometre branded as Maxxis. This is wonderful for TV exposure and media photographs.

In 2012, Rory Sutherland of the UnitedHealthcare Pro Cycling Team sponsored by Maxxis did his team and sponsor proud when he won the sixth stage of the race. Rory, originally from Australia but a resident of Boulder, Colorado, for several years, knew exactly how to pace himself for the last stretch of the stage, which finished with a tough climb. He took off over the last five kilometres to overtake everyone and win.

Rory Sutherland winning the sixth stage of the 2012 USA Pro Cycling Challenge in Boulder, Colorado. PHOTO CREDIT: JONATHAN DEVICH.

We have been a sponsor of the Amgen Tour of California, the largest professional cycling event in North America which combines world-class cycling with the beauty of California, from its very first tour in 2006. Apart from being the official automotive and bicycle tyre of the race, we also sponsored the Lifestyle Festivals offered in eight cities along the tour. Conducted by Health Net, each festival offered a health and fitness exhibition, cancer awareness education, tips on bicycle safety, etc. We also put on a performance by a BMX stunt team. The team dazzled spectators with gravity-defying tricks including back-flips, Supermans and 720s, which call for a cyclist to perform two 360-degree spins in mid-air.

The team we have been supporting for the Amgen Tour of California is the UnitedHealthcare Pro Cycling Team. It was known as the Health Net Pro Cycling Team Presented by Maxxis from 2003 to 2008, OUCH! Pro Cycling Team Presented by Maxxis in 2009,

(left) Aldo Ilesic and Jake Keough in the 2013 Tour of Langkawi in Malaysia. PHOTO CREDIT: JONATHAN DEVICH; (right) Geoff Kabush, 2012 Sea Otter Classic, Monterey, California. PHOTO CREDIT: RUMON CARTER.

and UnitedHealthcare Pro Cycling Team Presented by Maxxis from 2010. It is the same team that takes part in the USA Pro Challenge.

In 2012, Geoff Kabush represented Maxxis on the Canadian Scott-3Rox Racing Team. A Maxxis-sponsored athlete for many years, he is a three-time Olympian in mountain biking, seven-time Canadian mountain bike champion and the 2009 World Cup cross-country winner.

Kabush says that his time with Maxxis has been invaluable: "When I joined the Maxxis team in 2004, it really sparked my career and their support since has been incredible. It's been great to ride for a company like Maxxis that has a 100 per cent commitment to racing and performance at the highest level. Every weekend the mountain bike races I do are won and lost where the rubber meets the ground; wherever I am in the world, I always know Maxxis will have the perfect tyre to master the ever-changing conditions. Riding Maxxis tyres, I've had a record-setting number of wins, championships and national titles. Maxxis orange will always be a huge part of my identity as a racer and I'll always be grateful for everything they've contributed to my success as an athlete."

Women are not left out. We have sponsored Gunn-Rita Dahle Flesja, the Norwegian cross-country and marathon mountain biker who won the women's cross-country gold medal at the 2004 Olympic Games, six World Championships and six European championships. We also sponsor the Luna Pro Team, whose rider Georgia Gould won a bronze medal at the 2012 Olympic Games in London.

In Canada, we have hooked up with Crankworx Whistler, a ten-day mountain bike festival held in Whistler, British Columbia, which celebrates what it calls "epic endurance, supreme flow, monster air and vertical-dropping riding".

We are a silver level sponsor of the festival and the bike park at Whistler. We contribute money along with products which are used on the bike rentals and as prizes for the amateur races. In return, Crankworx recognises us as a sponsor on its website and in print advertising. We have signage throughout the Whistler Village during the mountain bike season, with additional exposure during the Crankworx festival. Our banners are out up along the course, our logos appear on kiosks around the village, and our inflatable tyre arch is used during some of the events.

The main event for the whole festival is the slope style competition, in which riders compete on a man-made course with huge jumps, drops and gaps. Winning the slope style competition is huge for a rider's career, not only because of the prize money, but because of the exposure it will give him or her. This is because virtually every mountain biking publication and website is present to watch the event. Unknown riders who have won the slope style competition have had their careers launched by it.

MIRACLE MIRRA

We were one of the sponsors of Dave Mirra, who has won more medals in the X Games, a yearly competition held for extreme sports athletes, than anyone else.

Mirra is a remarkable man and athlete. That's why we were associated with him. He became a professional BMX (bicycle motocross) rider in 1992, when he was only 17, and became quite successful until 1993, when he was hit by a drunk driver while crossing the street. He sustained a fractured skull and a torn shoulder, and had a blood clot in his brain. No one was sure if he would survive, but he pulled through. He then went through an excruciating period of recovery before he made it back to riding. By 1994, he had almost miraculously returned to his winning ways, coming out first in street and third in vert at the Chicago Bicycle Stunt Series competition.

From 1995, when the X Games was inaugurated, to 2008, he won medals every year. He is also involved in rally car racing and has been part of the Subaru Rally Team USA since 2010. Mirra assisted in the design of the Maxxis Miracle bicycle tyre with channelled tread to reduce rolling resistance. He used the tyre at two X Games and won gold medals at the events. Consumer feedback on the tyre has been excellent. One reviewer wrote he had been using the tyre "for about a year now" and it was, in his opinion, "one of the best". Elaborating further, he wrote: "I've taken it through rain and it grips like the road is dry … (The tyre) looks brand new as far as wear on the tread, and that's with riding 20+ miles every time I'm out."

BURNING RUBBER IN THE U.K.

In the U.K., we have a strong brand awareness campaign, sponsoring races and events. We have been the headline sponsor of the Maxxis

ACU British Motocross Championship without interruption since 2004. This is the main off-road competition in the U.K. for lightweight motorcycles with specialist frames and suspension. The ACU (Auto Cycle Union) is the governing body. Our support for the competition has enabled the brand to be seen worldwide through numerous media streams, including global TV coverage, with an estimated potential audience of 600 million.

The competition is organised mainly along the classes of MX1, for motorcycles from 251cc to 450cc, and MX2, for motorcycles from 175cc to 250cc. Our sponsorship involvement in these classes since 2001 has increased the tendency of racers to choose Maxxis tyres for their bikes. When we started, not many MX contestants would ride on a Maxxis tyre. We didn't have tyres that could complete at the highest level. But we worked with riders to find out what would work for them, and now we are among the top three in sales in the U.K. Our Maxxcross IT tyre is trusted by top MX teams. It features knobs designed to provide better handling and long wear. The rubber compound enhances stability and increases grip on any surface you can find on a motocross track or off-road loop.

Maxxis supports manufacturer teams like Apico Suzuki and Kawasaki by LPE, which has been going from strength to strength in the MX1 class since taking on two-time British champion Brad Anderson, riding a KX450F in both the Maxxis ACU British Motocross Championships and the Red Bull Pro Nationals. Anderson is joined by Darren Coutts and Connor Walkley.

We also have a presence in motorcycle road racing. In the British Superbike Championship, we supported the MSS Kawasaki team in 2010 and 2011, and Swan Yamaha in 2012. In 2013, we

Brad Anderson of Maxxis Kawasaki racing in the 2013 Maxxis British Motocross Championships.

signed with Milwaukee Yamaha, featuring British star rider James Ellison and Australian Josh Walters. In 2007, we were the headline sponsor of the British Supersport Championship, which is a support series to the British Superbike Championship providing opportunities for younger riders to step up to the latter. In 2008, we were named the official tyre partner for that year's Isle of Man TT Races.

AMBASSADOR WALKER

Someone who has become a brand ambassador for us is Chris Walker, a popular motorcycle road racer who has been a four-time runner-up in the British Superbike Championship and a race winner in the Superbike World Championship.

He started the unique Chris Walker Race School in 2012 which allows normal riders of all levels to live out their dreams on a closed circuit, riding Kawasaki ZX-R 600 machines under the instruction of Britain's fastest racers. The machines are all equipped with Maxxis MA-PS Sport tyres.

The school also proves the quality of products under all weather conditions, under extreme pressure, and it plays a significant part in helping Maxxis understand the way forward for the next generation. Chris also provides feedback on Maxxis' products both at his race school and his off-road motocross park, also founded in 2012. He attends U.K. shows, events and dealer open days where he teaches consumers about the benefits of Maxxis products.

BABES WITH BRAND BRIEFS

Our presence in the U.K. is also enhanced by our Maxxis Babes. These are bubbly and intelligent young women who grace the motor events, tyre exhibitions, races and competitions that we are involved in. They are carefully chosen to be our brand ambassadors. We have to ensure that they are photogenic, able to engage with people and, above all, able to engage with the Maxxis brand. They are taught everything they need to know about Maxxis so that they can answer questions about it from consumers. They are a massive crowd-puller, and people queue up to take photographs with them.

The equivalents of the Maxxis Babes in Latin America are known as Chica Maxxis, and in Malaysia as Maxxis Ambassadors. The Malaysian Ambassadors are given first-hand experience of testing Maxxis tyres under rugged conditions, such as in a rainforest. They go along with 4×4 drivers and rough it out to get to know what such a ride entails. This experience allows them to speak with authority when they answer consumers' questions at Maxxis events. The underlying idea is that the girls are not there just to attract crowds but to truly represent the Maxxis brand. They are trained on other aspects as well, briefed on all they need to know about Maxxis and tested on their knowledge of the brand afterwards. If they fail, they don't qualify.

(right) A Maxxis Ambassador, Malaysia; (below) Chica Maxxis from Latin America.

NO LESS
THAN 100%

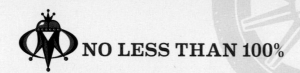

NO LESS THAN 100%

> If you think in terms of a year, plant a seed; if in terms of ten years, plant trees; if in terms of 100 years, teach the people.
>
> — Guanzi
>
> 一年之計，莫如樹穀；十年之計，莫如樹木；
> 百年之計，莫如樹人 (管子)

100% QUALITY. 100% SERVICE. 100% TRUST. These management goals make up the foundation of Maxxis. I came up with the Triple 3 value system for Maxxis in 2010. At the time, I strongly felt the need to express our corporate culture in a concrete form so that not only our employees but also our partners, suppliers, distributors and customers — in short, all our family members — could easily visualise the core principles that drive our company and our brand.

I also felt that once they understood these principles, our family members would embrace the values inherent in them and apply them in their daily Maxxis life. Triple 3 would serve as their guide as they went about their work, in dealing with customers, in promoting the Maxxis brand, or even in interactions among themselves.

Triple 3 reminds us that we must produce quality products — at all times. This is the responsibility of the R&D staff, the technical staff and the workers at the plants. We must keep this commitment as a sacred trust to ensure the safety of the people who buy and use our tyres. It is not merely a business priority; it is also a moral one. We don't believe in just making money out of business; we believe we must maintain our sense of humanity.

For quality control, we follow mainly the Japanese system, because the Japanese are highly respected for quality. Toyota also checks our quality periodically. Every tyre that we make goes through close inspection. But before any of those inspections take place, the mindset must be right at the manufacturing stage. As a Buddhist, I care about other people's lives, so I must make tyres with that caring attitude. Less importantly, this concern is also for my own job security and that of my employees, because if I supply tyres that are bad and frequently cause accidents, no one will want to buy them in the future.

So I Stress 100 Per Cent Quality.

To produce quality products, we must ensure that we provide the best service across the board. The R&D, technical and factory staff must give their best to ensure that the tyres we roll out every day meet and exceed the highest standards. Then, when it's time to market them, the sales and marketing teams must be up to speed in getting orders and delivering the goods to the satisfaction of the buyers. And when economic times are bad, the salespeople and our distributors must try even harder to maintain the orders, if not increase them further. This can be done if everyone gives their best.

SERVICE WITH A CUP OF TEA

At the retail level, dealers of our tyres will do better at their business if they build relationships with their customers and provide personal service. We encourage them to provide a comfortable rest area for their customers, engage in conversation with them, make them feel appreciated, and add a human touch to what would otherwise be a mechanical business transaction. In short, we encourage our dealers to provide their customers with the Maxxis experience that they cannot find elsewhere. It is somewhat like Starbucks, which is also in the service industry. This company offers its customers an experience. When you enter Starbucks, you want to feel the experience it offers. That's why you are willing to pay for its coffee, which costs more than that in regular coffee shops. The Starbucks coffee is not the main draw; the experience of being in Starbucks is — the experience of being in a home away from home.

We sell tyres, but we also try to create an experience for the customer — the experience of being more than just a customer. When you come to our store, we treat you like an old friend. In Chinese, we say: "溫馨的服務，永遠的朋友". We make you a long-time friend so you will trust us. You come to understand that we will not cheat you, and that trust should prompt you to keep buying from us.

WON SLOWLY, LOST QUICKLY

This brings me to the third component: Trust. It is something that is won slowly and can be lost quickly. We have to prove ourselves worthy of trust before we can earn it. And once we earn it, we must nurture it and preserve it.

Generally speaking, but also from the point of view of an employer, I believe we cannot get the best out of people if we don't

A poster of the Triple 3 concept.

trust them to show us what they can do. With our R&D and technical staff, for example, if we give them the trust to be as creative and innovative as possible, they will come up with excellent tyre designs, creative ways of mixing materials to form new compounds and new processes for efficient production. With our distributors, if we trust them to take care of their own regions, if we tell them that the Maxxis brand belongs to them as well, they will work even harder to promote Maxxis and bring in more orders. And if we trust them even further by not interfering with the way they work and not requiring quarterly sales statements from them or sending our own people from Taiwan to oversee their operations, they feel a greater sense of control and ownership, which translates into pride and stronger commitment.

Trust is particularly important, especially to a global company. Without trust, we would have to make constant checks to ensure that there are no errors, and this is not practical for a large company. With trust, we save time and costs.

We want our distributors to trust us. We encourage this trust by letting them know that we will not give distributorships to others as long as they meet our requirements. This way, they can go about their business without worrying about losing our business to local competitors. They will gain rewards for their investment.

At headquarters, we show by example that we abide by the management goals of quality, service and trust. This, in turn, motivates our partners to set the same goals for themselves. Headquarters has to be the role model. Then what we reflect will emanate to all our partners, all our family members, in all the places in the world to which we are connected.

Some of our dealers hang Triple 3 posters in their office to remind their employees to follow the management goals we have set. Even our suppliers do that. What's more, they instruct their employees to always be aware of the need to provide us with quality materials. That's excellent for us, because we can rest assured that we'll receive quality supplies. And this will naturally help us make quality products ourselves. Our suppliers know, of course, that if they serve us well and we produce tyres that are good and consequently sell well, it will benefit them too, because we will continue to give them business.

As Chun Yen Testing Machines Co. Ltd. is well aware, they have benefited from the fact that our business has continued to expand. As we grow, we keep asking them to design new machines for us. This helps them to grow as well. The relationship is mutually beneficial. They came in as our strategic partner because they trusted us, just as we trusted them to supply us with top-quality machines. This is the kind of trust we find meaningful and worthy of preserving. It's what keeps us both in business.

BUSINESS WITH HONOUR

Our mould-maker, Honor Well Mold Ind. Co. Ltd., in Beidou, Taiwan, started on a small scale with us in the early 1990s. Now, 95 per cent of its business is with us. In fact, our competitors are complaining that they can't get Honor Well to supply them with moulds because it is doing almost all its work for us. But business is business, and for Honor Well, business with us has been, as its president, Lin Hsi Tong, tells me, "like a family relationship".

Honor Well and Cheng Shin grew together over the years. Honor Well acknowledges that we are a good paymaster, which gives it the confidence and the resources to invest huge amounts in buying the required machinery. Before, it was producing small-sized tyre moulds, but as our needs grew and we needed larger moulds for our ATV and truck and bus tyres, it had to meet them by upgrading its technology. And it did so because of the trust built between us. We don't sign any contracts with Honor Well. If we want a new mould, we just issue a purchasing order. That's good enough for president Lin and his younger brother, Ming Hsi, who is the general manager. If we have problems with their moulds in our plant in Xiamen, they will promptly send their technicians there to troubleshoot. They try to measure up to the 100 per cent service we ask of them. And as for quality, we are satisfied that Honor Well provides us with top-class moulds. Otherwise, we would not have been buying from them for so long.

Honor Well has adopted the Triple 3 philosophy to use with its own stakeholders, a vivid example of both the power of this philosophy and our closeness to this company. Their use of Triple 3 has a double benefit for Honor Well: the firm gains by using a proven system and also works more easily with Maxxis, because both companies operate according to the same values. To commemorate our long-term positive relationship, we commissioned a plaque which names Honor Well a valued friend to Cheng Shin. Our relationship has an additional benefit for Honor Well: approval for loans is much easier because of the company's closeness to Cheng Shin.

All this shows that the whole business is, as I've said before, like a chain, and everyone is a vital link in the chain. Our chain is strong because Triple 3 reinforces the steel in our relationships, in the way we work with one another and relate to one another. In this way, not only do we cultivate a culture-rich and value-driven business but a human-based one as well.

WITH
TRIPLE 3,
EVERYBODY
WINS

WITH TRIPLE 3, EVERYBODY WINS

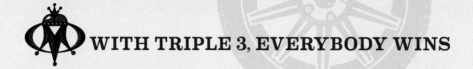

> Customers are jade, merchandise is grass.
>
> — Chinese proverb
>
> 以客為尊 (諺語)

I GOT MOST OF my ideas for Triple 3 from reading management books. Then with the help of Professor Stephen Chih-Yang Lu of the University of Southern California (USC), the ideas were visually rendered in the form of triangles within a larger triangle.

Professor Lu, who is Taiwanese, is a good friend. He is a leading internationally recognised authority on knowledge-based engineering systems. He obtained his first degree in mechanical engineering at National Taiwan University, and went on to obtain his M.S. and Ph.D. in the same field from the renowned Carnegie Mellon University in the U.S. He holds the David Packard Chair in manufacturing engineering at USC.

From time to time, he comes to Yuanlin to teach our employees Innovative Design Thinking. On the numerous occasions we had

The Triple 3 triangle.

met, I talked to him about my ideas. Later, I sent him a copy of my annual letter to our distributors in which I talked about the need to focus on quality, service and trust. He came back to me with a diagrammatic structure that systematised in visual terms what I had been thinking and talking about. I was amazed by it. It made the concepts so much more easily digestible. And he used as the core image a triangle, which appealed to me very much. A triangle is a striking image; we see how powerful it looks in the form of the great Egyptian pyramids. It is strong and durable, and therefore an apt symbol for our company.

Naturally, Professor Lu's diagram has become an iconic item of our company. We display it on the walls of our offices. We give posters of it to our strategic partners, our distributors, our retailers. We remind them that they are at the very centre of the triangle as part of what we call the "Maxxis Family".

Never Stop Innovating

For the Maxxis Family to be strong and prosperous, we must uphold the strategic objectives of being truly global, ensuring solid growth and being continuously innovative. All the three objectives are interconnected. I would say "either go global or go bankrupt".

We have to always come up with new products and improve on what we have done in order to secure solid sales that will make our company grow. Producing tyres is a complex business. It is labour-intensive, technology-intensive and capital-intensive. For us to maintain our place in this industry, we have to ensure that our revenue is substantial. We have to innovate all the time and create new products, or consumers will lose interest. The tyre business is not a "one size fits all" business.

(above) Dr Wally Chen with Thai dealers in a photo commemorating the first TBR tyre cured in Maxxis' second Thai plant, 2009; (left) Dr Chen signing the first tyre.

We are the biggest producer of bicycle and motorcycle tyres in the world. We make all kinds of tyres — for bicycles, motorcycles, passenger cars, trucks, buses, ATVs, sports utility vehicles (SUVs), armoured cars. And we have been busy innovating.

We produced the first truck and bus radial (TBR) tyre in Taiwan to serve the local market, so that these products no longer had to be imported from Japan. Now these tyres are sold all over the world. In an innovative touch, the carcasses of our TBR tyres are made of steel instead of the normal fibre. This allows them to be retreaded.

We invented the diamond-pattern tyres for motorcycles to provide a better grip when negotiating corners. The Supermaxx Diamond is used a lot by racing bikes.

We make all-steel radial tyres as well as bulletproof tyres for military use.

The U.S. National Aeronautics and Space Administration (NASA) has used our ATV Bighorn tyre in testing because it is strong enough to support the mass of the lunar vehicle and performs consistently.

The Supermaxx Diamond.

We came up with the first tubular tyre made in Taiwan, called the Maxxis Campione, suitable as well for bicycle racing. It has a dual-compound tread and a Kevlar® composite breaker to help prevent punctures. It also lowers rolling resistance and increases cornering grip.

We invented the first radial bicycle tyre in the world, called the Radiale. It gives a soft, smooth ride even on rough roads. It's ideal for racing.

We created the lightest bicycle tyre in the world called Maxxlite, weighing only 285 grams. It's also meant for racing.

The Bighorn.

Despite this record of achievement and innovation, we still need to grow. And to do that, we have to be truly global, which does not mean plain, simple globalisation. It means globalising our production, our marketing and our personnel. We have plants in various parts of the world that enable us to ship our products more efficiently and at lower costs to nearby regions. And for our marketing and our personnel, we rely on local people in various regions to market our products. We also rely on local personnel to run the business and clinch the deals. We don't need to send managers from Taiwan to make transactions.

This is globalisation combined with localisation, and it's far more effective than simple globalisation. It allows for the local dealers to take charge of the product and the brand, and make them their own. This combination gives them a sense of belonging to the global Maxxis family. This feeling translates into better sales and, therefore, more solid growth.

The Maxxlite.

When the company enjoys such growth, it will be inspired to innovate more. It will want to come out with better products, better designs for tyres. It will aim to be a market leader. So being truly global, ensuring solid growth and practising continuous innovation are part of a virtuous circle. That is why they are the three triangles surrounding the Maxxis Family. They are the core aims and business strategies that will maintain the happiness of the family.

Only the Best From Maxxis

To maintain these core aims and carry out our business strategies, we must uphold the key management goals of quality, service and trust. Naturally, these three form the triangles that are adjacent to the earlier three triangles of being truly global, ensuring solid growth and practising continuous innovation. And this also means that quality, service and trust encompass everyone in the Maxxis Family. It means that all of our stakeholders are also expected to set their sights on these goals whenever they engage in Maxxis business.

I say that 100 per cent is the standard for quality, service and trust because nothing can be better than 100 per cent. It also prevents other companies from using the same line because they will be seen to be copying Maxxis. More than that, 100 per cent distinguishes us from others: We pride ourselves on delivering the best. The rubber we buy for making our tyres is the best grade, regardless of the price we have to pay for it. And that standard holds true for all the tyres we make, regardless of the type, regardless of the brand. We do not buy inferior grades of rubber; they are not good enough for us.

When we say we deliver 100 per cent service, it means we provide the kind of service that nobody else provides. We rectify our errors immediately. If a customer points out a defect in our tyres, we attend to it without hesitation. We send our engineers out to listen to complaints so that they can come back and make improvements. Our engineers make the effort to explain to our distributors what our tyres are about so they know what they are selling.

Our dealers treat their customers as if they are part of the family, too, by serving them well, by showing them hospitality, by engaging with them on a personal level instead of seeing them as mere business digits. This is how trust is earned. And since our aim is to secure as well as give 100 per cent trust, we have to think of relationships as being long-term.

Surrounding the triangle for trust are the three smaller triangles of local customer, strategic partner and honest employee.

We aim to develop loyal customers who will buy Maxxis from the time they are introduced to our brand as well as those who start using our bicycle tyres as children, and grow up to ride motorcycles and eventually drive cars. We cultivate strategic partners with whom we can work and share knowledge and prosperity. The trust between us is mutual to ensure a partnership that is lasting and fruitful. We welcome honest employees who intend to stay with the company for a long time and consider Maxxis their home. Indeed, we have many employees who have stayed with us for 10, 20 and even 30 years. As the years have passed, the children of some long-time employees have come to work with the company, such that our relationship spans two generations.

NURTURE RELATIONSHIPS WITH YOUNG CUSTOMERS

For all three categories, we have to start by earning trust. For customers, we first cater to the young by providing them with quality bicycle tyres. We like to say we make friends with young people, so that when they grow up, they are already familiar with Maxxis. Then, when they buy motorcycle or car tyres, they will be comfortable buying Maxxis, a familiar and trusted brand.

This strategy requires us to build our brand. We have to let people know why our brand of tyres is of high quality. We have to impress on the public that our brand has a high profile, so we participate in sponsorships. We create the impression that we are a big player by associating ourselves with big and successful teams.

China trusts brands, and they trust ours — both the Cheng Shin and Maxxis brands. That is why we are Number One in China in bicycle and motorcycle tyre sales. Overall, we are also the top tyre-maker in the Greater China market that covers Taiwan as well as China and Hong Kong.

China trusts us also because of the quality of our tyres. Related to quality are producing the best product, applying the right and moral work ethics, and striving for continuous improvement. I have already touched on our purchase of the best grade of rubber to produce the best product. In terms of work ethics, we always keep in mind the safety of our consumers to drive us to make tyres that will be safe for them to use. This awareness of safety is interconnected with producing the best product. Both are dependent on each other. If you don't have the moral will to produce tyres that are safe for use, you will not produce the best product. Our moral compass gives us that impetus. And because we want to make the best product, we are dedicated to the task of continuous improvement. Everything works together in each of the triangle formations. Everything is integrated.

Everybody Wins

This integrated approach also informs our attitude towards service. We emphasise trust-based selling because this kind of selling will be lasting and therefore brings everyone lifetime benefits. If a dealer makes his customer a friend, the relationship will be based on trust and lasts longer than if he treats the latter as simply a source of profit. This is the same example we set when we deal with our distributors. We don't talk price all at once, we don't ask them how many tyres they are going to take from us at the start. We talk about how we can mutually benefit from working together, we talk about the viability of our brand. We don't micromanage by asking them to furnish us with quarterly performances; we leave them to do what they do best.

We ask them to be our brand ambassadors. We ask them to embrace our brand as their own. They take pride in this trust and sense of partnership, and work hard at promoting the brand. And if they continue to do well at it, the brand will be theirs for a lifetime. If theirs is a family business, they can pass it on to their children. We welcome that, and we welcome their children into the Maxxis Family. This has worked so well most of the time that a distributor once told me, "To be a Maxxis distributor and not make money is a disgrace."

As brand ambassadors, our distributors voluntarily share their fruitful Maxxis experiences with friends and potential prospects. One such distributor in Mexico spent four long hours on the phone telling a new prospect about the benefits he had derived from working with Maxxis and the success he had achieved. Both their wives got suspicious; they thought their husbands were talking to other women! In any case, the conversation convinced the new prospect to make an investment and come in with Maxxis. A few years later, he abandoned other brands and concentrated exclusively on our products. He has certainly not regretted this decision. Since 2006, he has become the Number One car tyre importer in his country.

On the dealers' part, they can make brand ambassadors of their customers by giving them the kind of service that others don't give. If their service is 100 per cent, their customers will let others know about it, and this will bring in new customers. Over time, when people associate 100 per cent service with Maxxis, this will bring untold benefits to all concerned. Everyone will win, including Maxxis.

TRIPLE 3
IN
ACTION

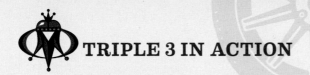

TRIPLE 3 IN ACTION

> The superior man understands what is right; the inferior man understands what will sell.
>
> — Kung Fu-tzu
>
> 君子喻於義，小人喻於利 (孔子)

TRIPLE 3 IS NOT SOMETHING I have formulated merely as a philosophical guide. It is something we put into practice.

To make our staff aware of it and inculcate in them the importance of practising the desired principles in their daily work, our vice-president for culture building and branding, Tony Huang, conducts classes on Triple 3. That investment of time shows how serious we are about this philosophy. Also, it is very rare that a company creates a job designation like Tony's; most businesses don't even think of culture building.

Tony teaches Triple 3 to several levels of the staff, from group leaders to section chiefs to managers. They, in turn, will teach it to their colleagues. He also goes to our distributors to share Triple 3 with them. Some of them have come back to tell us that knowing the concepts has benefited their business.

Among the staff, Tony has seen changes in their social conduct after teaching the component on work ethics, which is related to the management goal of quality. Before the training, the participants did not care to greet their colleagues when they saw one another. But after a few sessions of being educated on work ethics, they began to do it as a matter of habit. Tony noticed that they also began to dress more appropriately. And they were more conscious of presenting the company in a positive light by, for example, making it a point to wear a helmet when they were out riding a bicycle while attired in company uniform.

More significantly, the staff became more conscious of the need to treat safety as a priority and to be more careful in their work. They realised that if we sold tyres that were defective, people could get hurt, even killed, in accidents. And these could even be their own relatives if they were consumers using these tyres.

On service, there are many things a worker — or a dealer — can do to fulfil that management goal. For instance, if someone drives her car to a tyre dealer's shop to have the pressure of her tyres checked, it would be a demonstration of good service if the dealer checked the pressure of the customer's spare tyre as well.

OUR CLOCKWORK TEA LADY

These are things we don't have to teach specifically. Knowing the principles is enough for each individual to find the appropriate ways of showing good service. I like to give the example of our tea lady, who is responsible for serving tea or coffee to visitors who come to our office in Yuanlin. She is aware that we want our visitors to feel welcome, so she makes sure she refills their cups hourly. To remind herself, she sets an alarm for every hour. This allows her to appear like clockwork, so to speak. I did not give her any instructions on how to do this; she thought of the idea herself. She knows what service is all about.

Our engineers have also been known to provide service in an extraordinary case. This was for a policeman and his wife who went around riding a tandem bicycle. The policeman was quite heavy; he weighed about 90 kilos. His wife weighed about 60 kilos. The tyres of their bicycle would usually last them about a week before they gave way under the couple's combined weight.

The couple was recommended by a friend to try Maxxis tyres, and so they did. They were happy to discover that the Maxxis tyres lasted a month. But the policeman then decided to see if the Maxxis tyres would last even longer than that, so he kept using them beyond a month. One day, the tyres blew up, and the man fell. He was slightly injured on his face. So he sent a letter to our company to describe what had happened. Our engineers went to see him and to have a look at the damage. They told him the tyres were not designed for his purpose. Then they came back and designed one that would suit him better. He was astonished, thrilled and grateful that we specifically designed a special tyre just for him.

GOING THE EXTRA MILE

Once in a while, Tony brings in someone from outside the company to add new perspective in our training. One such person was a flight attendant sent by China Airlines to talk about providing good service. She took the high-speed train from south Taiwan to Taichung, and we were supposed to pick her up from there. But before she arrived, we

A plaque dedicated to the employees of Maxxis' North American headquarters in Suwanee, Georgia.

got a call from her saying that she would be late due to a potentially serious situation which had arisen concerning her health.

When she arrived, we called the hospital near our factory to say we were bringing someone in for treatment and took her straight there. We have good relations with the hospital's director, who is my ex-classmate. Apart from donating money to this hospital, I send employees there for treatment.

Our good relationship with the hospital meant that when we arrived, a physician was already prepared to see to her. If not for our connection with the hospital, she would have had to wait a long time. After the medical examination, she was able to come to our office with ample time to give her talk. She was overwhelmed with emotion when she acknowledged that she had come to provide service but, as it had turned out, we were the ones providing her with excellent care and service. She said we didn't need any training on service at all!

I have to say she's quite right. Especially among our employees who have been with us for some time, the spirit of serving and helping others is well ingrained. They have internalised the company culture and made service their way of life. They will go to extra lengths to make sure the customer is satisfied or that things work out all right.

For instance, a few years ago, some Taiwan dealers wanted to visit Disneyland. To help facilitate their visa applications, we got Maxxis International USA to send them letters of invitation to visit our office there. As Maxxis is a known company in the U.S., such an invitation helps to influence approval of visa applications. Sure enough, the dealers got their visas and happily headed for Disneyland.

During the course of their visit, however, one of them, a woman, went missing. As Disneyland is huge and packed with thousands of people, the others in her group couldn't find her. And none of them knew her mobile number. Fortunately, we had one of our staff, Lai Ming Hor from the Domestic Sales Department in Taiwan, accompanying them, and he knew the woman's husband who was, at the time, in Taiwan. So he called the man and got his wife's mobile number from him. Then he called the woman to find out where she was in Disneyland! It was a roundabout way of locating a person — going halfway round the globe to do it, so to speak — but it did the job. And it reflected well on our company and the dedication of our employees.

At other times, we help out of humanitarian concern, as we did for a relative of one of our Taiwan distributors when he got into a serious accident while holidaying in Chiengmai, Thailand.

He and his wife were being driven around the mountainous countryside there when their vehicle fell into a ravine. His wife was all right, but he was severely injured because he was so preoccupied with taking photos that he had neglected to wear a seat belt. When he was taken to a hospital, the doctors discovered he had suffered paralysis from the neck down. His wife was in despair because there was no one in Chiengmai who could help them. They did not have enough money with them either. She remembered that we had a plant in Thailand, so she called our Taiwan distributor, who then called Leonard Liao, our senior manager in the Domestic Sales Department.

Liao contacted our Thailand office, and the next day one of our Taiwanese staff stationed in Thailand went to visit the injured man in the Chiengmai hospital. Acting on our instructions, he paid the hospital bills, much to the surprise of the man's wife. Then, he helped arrange for the couple to be flown back to Taiwan.

Money is Not the Issue

Doing things like this defines who we are. For us, money is not the issue in any relationship. What's important is touching other people's hearts and improving lives.

In July 2011, during the monsoon season, huge parts of Thailand were crippled by severe floods. About 13.6 million people were affected and 815 died. In some areas, the floods did not subside until January 2012. We helped by donating essential items to the local communities.

In November 2012, an earthquake that registered a massive 7.5 on the Richter scale struck Guatemala, killing at least 48 people. It was the worst earthquake to hit that country since 1976. The hardest-hit area was the province of San Marcos, where 40 people died. We got together with some of our Latin America distributors to raise US$26,800 to buy essential foodstuff for the victims. The Taiwan

Dr Wally Chen enjoying a day out on Taiwan's Peng-Hu Islands during a visit with local distributors, May 2012.

Embassy in Guatemala and the Buddhist Tzu Chi Foundation joined us in giving out donations to 2,200 families in the municipality of San Pedro Sacatepéquez.

In Taiwan, we give out lunch boxes regularly to the poor living near our factory. In the U.S., we give out scholarships to the best and second best students graduating from public high schools in Gwinnett County, Georgia, where Maxxis USA is located. Begun in 2004, these scholarships are typically awarded to at least 44 students. Money from the scholarships can be used to defray post-secondary education expenses including books, housing or other school-related needs.

It's not just about corporate social responsibility. It's about taking care of communities that mean something to us.

TOUCHING
LIVES,
MAKING
SUCCESSES

TOUCHING LIVES, MAKING SUCCESSES

> When the best leader's work is done, the people say: 'We did it ourselves.'
>
> — Lao Tzu
>
> 功成事遂，百姓皆謂："我自然"（老子）

MAXXIS HAS TOUCHED MANY LIVES. It has also touched ours — in unexpected ways. One of the most poignant instances was when Lenny Lee visited Cairo on May 28, 2010, months before the Arab Spring.

At the time, Egypt was just a small market for us. And this was Lenny's first visit to our distributor there. He had no idea of the reception he was going to get. When his plane landed, he was surprised to find the distributor waiting to pick him up from the airport. He had not expected this. He was grateful for the hospitality and happily got into the car provided. But what he saw next as the car pulled out of the airport road made his heart jump for joy.

Following behind was a convoy of a hundred taxis, each bearing the Maxxis logo!

He was driven to the iconic Tahrir Square where, to his amazement and wonder, another 150 taxis were waiting, each with the Maxxis logo on it as well! Surrounding them was a festive abundance of Maxxis banners. But that was not all. The taxis were arranged in such a manner that from a bird's eye view, they formed the word "Maxxis". The only thing they couldn't do was slot a car into the horizontal stroke of the letter "A" because the space was probably too tight!

Lenny was so overwhelmed with emotion at the sight of it all that tears came to his eyes. At that moment, he felt prouder of Maxxis and Taiwan than he had ever felt before.

He marvelled at the huge amount of work that must have been put into welcoming him. It made him realise that the distributor wanted to show him how hard they had been promoting Maxxis. The Maxxis advertisement in the Cairo tourist guide was another indication of this distributor's effort.

Business in Egypt has since been growing steadily, at about 30 per cent a year. It did suffer a drop during the tumultuous period of the Egyptian Revolution that led to the downfall of then-Egyptian president Hosni Mubarak. But even during a revolution, life and transportation had to go on. And so tyres needed replacing. When things settled down, the business began picking up again, and our Egyptian distributor is getting along fine.

In fact, we are doing very well in the Middle East. Thanks to Taiwan's neutrality, we are also selling in Iran and Iraq. In 2012, sales in Iran went up 37 per cent. When our sales team visited Iraq, they were taken to a street where almost every tyre shop displayed a Maxxis signboard. To provide better service to our customers in the Middle

Executives and staff of Maxxis' distributor
in Egypt at the 2010 Egypt taxi show.

Maxxis stores in Kuwait (top) and Jordan.

A Maxxis store in Jeddah, Saudi Arabia.

East and Africa, we opened an office in Dubai in the United Arab Emirates in 2007. It handles sales, marketing and customer service.

The tyre market is really huge, especially in emerging countries where there is an increasing need for transportation for all kinds of purposes — and transportation requires tyres. That is why we have been expanding aggressively in these areas.

Sri Lanka has been good to us. When I came out with Triple 3 and we promoted it there, the Sri Lanka distributor promised to put up 100 Maxxis signboards throughout the country. They have since kept their promise, and sales in Sri Lanka have been going up every year. These examples show that if people are loyal to a brand, they will work hard for it.

Latin America Breakthrough

We have also touched many lives in Latin America. We introduced Maxxis there in 1997, starting mainly with car tyres. Mexico was the first market that we entered. Before this, the Cheng Shin brand was already known in the Latin American market for bicycle and motorcycle tyres; in fact, they accounted for more than 90 per cent of the total sales in the region until the late 1990s. Now the sales structure in Latin America has completely changed; Maxxis car tyres account for 70 per cent of total sales in Latin America, and Maxxis is one of the top leading brands there in that category.

I made Paul Huang our sales director in charge of Latin America. He runs it from Dallas, where we have our head office for Latin American sales and marketing. He has been carrying out a spectrum of branding activities, including sponsoring a few World Cup qualifying matches involving the teams under CONCACAF (Confederation of North, Central American and Caribbean Association Football), the Lorena Ochoa Invitational part of the LPGA in Mexico, a car exhibition in Peru, the Autocross Honduras, the Argentine Cross Country Rally Championship, the World Enduro Championship which is popular among off-road motorcyclists, and many more. He has covered every country in the continent. He even organises a Maxxis Girl Contest that has turned out to be very popular.

In the beginning, some distributors in Latin America took to Maxxis when they were still small operations or when they were looking for breakthroughs in the tyre industry. For example, a company in Ecuador that specialised in motorcycle parts and accessories, including tyres, faced difficulties in growing its business. Paul helped the owners to do a market survey and gave them the option to expand into the competitive market of selling car tyres. He offered them Maxxis. They

Maxxis SuperB Dakar Team in Peru, 2013.

were hesitant because they knew little about the car tyre market. They were also worried that it was already too competitive. Paul assessed the situation and evaluated the company, then proposed a sales strategy and market introduction plan. He worked closely with the company in developing a niche market, building a product portfolio, visiting shops, organising shipping arrangements and so on. After a few years, the company became the biggest importer of car tyres in Ecuador.

No Emerging Market Too Hard to Enter

Lenny opened new markets in Indonesia and some countries in Africa, and the sales have been good. We spend money promoting our brands in Nigeria and South Africa by sponsoring billboards and local football tournaments. Lenny goes around to talk to tyre shop owners and their tyre-fitters and also end-users to get first-hand information on what they think of our tyres. In Nairobi, Kenya, taxi drivers told him that Maxxis tyres were the ones that worked best for long-distance driving.

The Indonesia market has plenty of potential because the population is huge and the demand for tyres is phenomenal. Before Lenny went to sell Maxxis in Indonesia, our tyres were not available there at all. Indonesia was then a closed market and as its local tyre manufacturing was also quite strong, we thought that as a Chinese company, we would be at a disadvantage, but we were wrong. The results have been very promising.

We are looking at additional emerging markets to enter. Pricing is of course very important, but we don't only negotiate the best price; we get our people to visit the market to understand its needs and the overall situation there. We gauge which of our broad range of tyres would be suitable for the market. There is no emerging market so far that is too difficult for us to penetrate. If you were to ask Lenny what the toughest market is, he would say, "None, really."

To help us grow, we have to be thorough and careful in choosing our distributors. It's not difficult for us to find distributors because we are ninth in the world; many distributors want to come in with us. But it's important to select the right partners. We study their company profile and financial standing. Experience in dealing with tyres is preferred but not essential, because they can always find experts on the tyre business in their local market. We look at their business plan for us. We try to get a sense of their marketing and branding aptitude, as well as their affinity for the Maxxis culture. On this score, one important consideration for us is their family background, because Maxxis is itself a family.

Once we sign a distributor, we give them exclusive rights to our brands. We make visits to see how they are doing, have annual meetings with them, monitor their sales and observe how they build brand awareness. Most of the time, our selections have turned out

Dr Wally Chen with Australian distributor during his visit to Australia, January 2013.

well, and we find distributors who have worked long-term and happily with us — and of course, they've made a lot of money.

ASIAN & AFRICAN DISTRIBUTOR CONFERENCE

Their happy relationship with Maxxis was evident at the second Maxxis Asian & African Distributor Conference held in Penang, Malaysia, in June 2013. Apart from building a strong feeling of camaraderie with everyone present, the participants from the two regions shared valuable information about their marketing strategies, warehouse management and experiences selling Maxxis products. As we learned from one another, we felt that everyone was committed to the cause of growing together. We felt like a big, united community not only of businesspeople but of human beings, experiencing the real power of the Maxxis family. Many of the participants wrote to me afterwards to say how much they appreciated meeting up at the conference. They also said they were eagerly looking forward to the next one.

Dr Wally Chen with VIPs from ExxonMobil at the 2013 Maxxis Asian & African Distributor Conference.

Cultural night at the conference.

Participants at the Asian & African Distributor Conference in Penang.

STRAIGHT TO THE TOP IN BANGLADESH

Swan International, based in Dhaka, has been our sole distributor for Bangladesh since 1996. Their network is extensive and they have more than 160 dealers throughout the country.

They started out selling the Cheng Shin brand of light truck and bus tyres and then passenger car tyres. But now they sell our Maxxis, CST and Pressa brands as well as Cheng Shin. They have also expanded their range to include bicycle, motorcycle and other kinds of tyres.

Before they came on board with us, no one in Bangladesh was selling tyres from Taiwan. And when they started to do so, they had a hard time convincing customers. People would say, "Taiwan? That's China. Forget it!" But Swan International worked hard to prove to them the quality of our tyres and managed to change minds. Now, since 2010, Maxxis has been Number One in Bangladesh.

For their hard work, between 1996 and 2008, Swan International achieved a growth of 1,000 per cent. And from 2008 to 2012, they managed to score a100 per cent annual increase in sales. In 2011, they recorded sales of US$16 million. In 2012, when most of the world was stuck in the economic doldrums, the figure rose to more than US$20 million, up 26 per cent.

Swan International chairman Mohammed Shahabuddin tells us this is mainly because of the quality of our tyres. As an example, he says, the trucks in his country tend to be overloaded; the operators may be allowed a load capacity of 15 tons, but they take on 25 to 30 tons and for that, they need Maxxis tyres. No other tyres would be able to take that kind of pressure. This level of durability has been tried and tested.

Mohammed Shahabuddin and his son, Amzad Khan, who is Swan International's brand manager, also do a lot to promote the Maxxis brand, even though this added promotion incurs high costs. They take their cue from us about the need for branding, so they try to convince their dealers to invest in Maxxis' branding efforts. Among their many clever promotional items is a Maxxis watch which they specially created as an incentive gift to customers.

On the whole, we are very pleased with our relationship with Swan International. They, in turn, are very pleased that we are the only manufacturer in the world that provides such a broad range of tyres, and that we are the only manufacturer in the world that allows its dealers to sell all of our brands.

THE TYRES LAST LONGER

In Malaysia, we have a healthy and happy relationship with Kian Hon, our sole distributor for tyres for all vehicles except two-wheeled types, which are the exclusive domain of Daytona Sport Trading. Kian Hon is based in the north of the country, in Nibong Tebal, Penang, whereas Daytona is in the south, in Johor Baru, Johor.

Daytona joined us in 2006 to sell Cheng Shin and Maxxis bicycle and motorcycle tyres. As Swan International experienced, when they started, it was not easy. They tried to sell Maxxis tyres, but we were not well-known in Malaysia and the prices were high. Customers were somewhat familiar with Cheng Shin tyres, but they were reluctant to buy them because they also said, "Taiwan? That's China. No good." Fortunately, Tan Kiat, the man behind Daytona, has the same concept of trust as Maxxis. He let his customers take a small number of tyres to try out, without demanding that they pay first. When they did the testing, they found the tyres were good and came back to make orders.

In Johor Baru, a lot of people commute to Singapore on a daily basis to work there or engage in some kind of activity or other. Going there and back, commuters cover a distance of about 100 kilometres, and an estimated 100,000 motorcycles make the trip daily. The motorcyclists found that with a different brand of tyres, they needed to change after three months, but with Cheng Shin tyres, they could stretch them for as long as five. Pretty soon, in about a year, the sales of Cheng Shin tyres improved.

The next challenge was to increase the demand for Maxxis tyres. Before 2006, Daytona was doing business only in the southern part of the country. When we signed them, we requested that they expand their business nationwide. After one year, we were aware that they were not buying many Maxxis tyres from us because they were not making money from them, so I decided to give them US$33,000 to sponsor the Petronas Malaysian Cup Prix Championship, a national-level underbone racing series for motorcycles with displacements from 115cc to 130cc. I thought that this sponsorship would help them make Maxxis better known to motorcycle riders. The competitors in this championship could be as young as 13 years old because there are numerous categories in this series, and we believe in getting people to familiarise themselves with our products from a young age. Furthermore, there were ten rounds to the championship, and each round was held in a different part of the country. This geographic diversity was useful for extending our brand exposure.

Tan was very receptive to the idea of promoting the brand through sponsorships because he had the same idea. And he was rather surprised that I was willing to help with sponsorship money, even though he had not been giving us much business. I saw this financial contribution as a way to give a boost to a family member in order to get the business going. As it turned out, more people did become aware of Maxxis through our sponsorship of the racing series. When they saw that we could do well for racing tyres, they realised we would also do well for general-use tyres.

Then in 2011, a club called Kommuniti Permotoran Utara (Northern Motoring Community) wanted to set a Malaysian record for going around the country in 24 hours. Months before they set off, the club tried out a number of tyre brands. They eventually chose Maxxis. They said they needed tyres that could endure the hot weather and intermittent rain along the way — and ours would. They were right. When they completed their gruelling journey, after having covered a distance of 2,319 kilometres, the tyres still had their treads intact. They were worn, but still highly visible. The experience of this club showed that Maxxis tyres give greater mileage.

That piece of information is now included in Daytona's

promotional materials and insertions in bike magazines. Such promotion, combined with Tan's management capabilities and hard work, has paid off handsomely. From 2007 onwards, Daytona has been enjoying double-digit growth. In 2012, its sales went up 40 per cent. Now Daytona commands 20 per cent of the market share in Malaysia for the highest-grade category of tyres. Most Malaysian bikers regard either Maxxis or Michelin as their first choice.

The service Daytona provides helps to account for its booming business. To ensure that they deliver orders on time, the company makes good use of the newest electronic technology available. Daytona was the first tyre distributor in the southern region of Malaysia to go online to see to customer needs. Tan supplies his salespeople with personal digital assistants (PDAs) so that they can email orders immediately when they are in other parts of the country. Otherwise, the ordering process could take as long as three to five days. He also instructs his salespeople to send their orders in every day.

Tan tells us that he usually hears complaints about products rather than positive feedback, but for Maxxis tyres, customers actually express their appreciation. They often say that using Maxxis means they don't have to change their tyres so frequently. This has motivated Tan's dealers to stock up with mostly Maxxis tyres; in the past, they carried an assortment of other brands as well.

People who ride motorcycles fitted with sidecars go for Maxxis because our tyres can take the heavier load and last longer. According to Tan's feedback, other tyres can last 30 days for these vehicles, but ours last 45. News vendors also prefer Maxxis because the newspapers they carry exert a heavy strain on their motorcycle tyres, and our tyres can handle the added load.

The Sky is the Limit

Kian Hon has been with us since 2006. Its chairman, Tan Yang Nam, often tells me how grateful he is to Maxxis and that we are a kind of corporate elder brother to Kian Hon. It's true, we have a good relationship. And we trust each other.

In 2012, Kian Hon opened its new building, in which it has invested a great deal of money, and dedicated part of it to a training centre named after Maxxis. This new facility has meaning beyond its more obvious uses. It says that Kian Hon is expanding, and that the company is confident it will achieve greater success with expansion, much of which was brought about by Kian Hon's association with Maxxis.

We were not told in advance that Kian Hon was going to invest in this new building and training centre. When we found out, we were pleasantly surprised. Investing so much in this new development shows the trust Yang Nam and his partner, Tan Yeang Siang, who is also his brother and the company's chief financial officer, have in us.

On their part, they appreciate our willingness to send our engineers to their plant to transfer knowledge and, more importantly, listen to their complaints about defects in our tyres. They like the fact that we are concerned enough to collect information that will help us improve our products. They tell us that this is unfortunately not the case with other big tyre-makers, who do not routinely visit and talk to them on such a personal level. And when it comes to explaining their latest products, they will typically just send a PowerPoint and request that it be channelled to Kian Hon's network. We send the very engineers involved in designing the new products to give presentations and take enquiries, not only from Kian Hon but also its dealers.

Lion dance at Kian Hon's new office during the 2013 conference in Penang. (top, from left to right) Maxxis USA president James Tzen, Kian Hon's managing director Sydney Tan, Dr Wally Chen and Lenny Lee; (bottom) James Tzen and Dr Wally Chen.

Kian Hon also appreciates our keeping our word in not contracting any other distributor in Malaysia and in allowing them to be called Maxxis Malaysia even though Kian Hon is not our subsidiary. This gives them added confidence in our relationship, which helps them to conduct their business.

Kian Hon has done a good job of identifying the categories of tyres which will sell well in Malaysia. They include tyres for mountain bikes, dirt bikes, ATVs and 4×4s. Kian Hon is now trying to make our 4×4 tyres Number One in the country.

In the meantime, they have been actively promoting the Maxxis brand by putting up billboards along the North-South Expressway, reminding people that we are ninth among tyre-makers in the world.

Kian Hon also promotes our sponsorship of the Liverpool English football club, which has many Malaysian fans, by producing Liverpool banners for use at events and photo shoots.

One of the many things I admire about Kian Hon is its adeptness at tapping into social media. The club has several thousand dedicated followers. Kian Hon recorded its own visuals from tests of our 4×4 tyres, which they conducted themselves and placed on the club's Facebook page. The Facebook presence proved to be a good way to generate reactions to products and interesting questions from fans, and therefore develop a niche for the brand. This strategy is turning out to be more effective than the hard-sell approach.

The Maxxis 4×4 Club also participated in a travelogue in collaboration with a TV channel on how to go into extreme terrain with a mildly modified vehicle and inexperienced drivers, and come out safely without damage to the vehicle. Its next project — a big one — will be the prestigious Rainforest Challenge, an off-road tourism event that takes 4×4 enthusiasts on a tough adventure in the jungle. This project was launched in Malaysia in 1997 but is now organised in other parts of the world as well. Closely watched by the motoring, lifestyle, off-road and adventure media from around the world, it gives good exposure to everyone involved. For us, the exposure of the Maxxis name will be valuable, without our even having to spend money in terms of sponsorship.

I wholeheartedly agree with Kian Hon's approach of spending $1 to get back $10 in its branding efforts. This is the same approach I take in regard to Maxxis' own global branding, for example, when it comes to sponsoring the big baseball and basketball teams in the U.S. I try to get maximum effect from minimum spending. In Kian Hon's case, this strategy translates to an understanding that merely putting advertisements in magazines is not spending money wisely; Kian Hon ensures they get a write-up as well. This gives more substance and added exposure to the branding effort.

I think much of the credit for Kian Hon's dynamism should go to its managing director, Sydney Tan. A graduate of Emory University in the U.S., she is a bright young spark who often comes to us with good ideas. We treat her like a real member of the family and have given her a position as Asia marketing consultant for Maxxis. She speaks from a consumer's point of view, which aligns with my belief in the power of customer feedback. She is also constantly emphasising the importance of exploiting new media to project ourselves and find out about market trends. Using new platforms for our message helps us break away from our traditional way of doing things. I find it very refreshing.

THE AUSPICIOUS TRIPLE 12

On December 12, 2012, Kian Hon held the official opening of its new building. The grand event, dubbed "Triple 12" because of the date, was attended by a few hundred guests, including Maxxis family members from overseas. They came from Japan, Thailand, Indonesia, Singapore, Bangladesh, China and, of course, Taiwan.

Together with Yang Nam, I lit the firecrackers to inaugurate the event. The deafening bursts that resulted were meant to chase away evil spirits so that good luck would stay with Kian Hon — and Maxxis. For this was, in a way, a celebration for us, too, as the event symbolised a partnership between our two companies aimed at boosting our presence in Malaysia and Asia. The new three-storey building would not just be for Kian Hon's use; it would also be the home of the Maxxis Asia Truck and Bus Radial Education Centre (MATEC), which will help facilitate training and exchange of ideas

Dr Wally Chen at a press conference in Penang with the chief executive for the Northern Corridor Implementation Authority (NCIA) Malaysia, Mr. Dato' Redza Rafiqat, October 2012. Maxxis was there to set up MATEC.

and information among Maxxis' Asian family members on truck and bus radial technology. Distributors could come to this space, where Maxxis engineers and experts and other speakers invited from all over the world could share their knowledge. Distributors, in turn, could share their experiences of the buying behaviour in their respective countries. We plan to develop an integrated database of information that will be useful for all of us in our drive to improve our products and marketing.

This is the kind of strategic partnership that Maxxis advocates. Simultaneously, we have a strategic partnership with Kian Hon to expand retreading operations, an area in which Kian Hon has had much experience. The new building will also house a tread rubber production line, an extension of Kian Hon's existing retreading plant. This new facility will allow increased production of retreaded tyres to a full capacity of 120,000 units per year.

This is a win-win arrangement for both companies. With the contemporary emphasis on recycling, we foresee that retreading is likely to be a big enterprise in the near future. It will reduce oil dependency by 70 per cent and pollution from tyre disposal by 80 per cent. For the consumer, buying a retread is 30 to 50 per cent cheaper than buying a new tyre. Since Kian Hon has had more than 30 years of experience in the retread business and we have been producing tyres that are of a quality that is conducive to retreading after their initial tread life ends, it is only natural for us to work together to be more efficient and also environmentally responsible.

The arrangement we have is actually based on a frugal business model. Each contributes what it does best and with its available resources. There is no extra expense, as such. Maxxis is able to mix the rubber and provide it to Kian Hon because we have the available resources to do so. This process is technology- and capital-intensive, and therefore, too expensive for Kian Hon to undertake. Kian Hon takes the rubber from us, does the necessary retreading and sells the tyres to its established clientele. If Maxxis were to set up its own retread business from scratch, it would almost certainly take a few years to get it off the ground and at much greater expense. If Kian Hon were to make its own treads, it would have to invest a great deal. With this collaboration, we avoid the risks that come with new investments, and we both benefit.

At the Triple 12 ceremony, we sanctified the collaboration with a number of rituals. After setting off the firecrackers, we had a lion dance. First, the lion greeted me and Yang Nam to give its blessing. Then it proceeded to jump onto the lined-up stilts, each one progressively higher than the last, with the highest standing 10 feet tall. As it danced to the beat of drums and the clashing of cymbals,

Triple 12's ribbon cutting ceremony on December 12, 2012. From left to right are the chairman of Kian Hon, Mr. Tan Yang Nam; deputy foreign minister, Ministry of Foreign Affairs, Malaysia, Mr. Y.B. Senator A. Kohilan Pillay; Dr Wally Chen; and the managing director of SIRIM QAS International Sdn. Bhd., Ms. Khalidah Mustafa.

Firecrackers to chase away evil spirits at the Triple 12 event.

The "Maxxis balcony", an intricately designed stainless steel structure dedicated to Kian Hon at the Triple 12 event.

and leaped with perfect synchronisation between two dancers, from one stilt to another, going ever upwards, I saw the lion as a metaphor for Maxxis' own performance in the tyre industry. I was heartened by the display. I was told afterwards that the troupe performing the dance was the world champion, and I wasn't surprised. They were the best I had ever seen.

This was followed by a dragon dance, symbolising more good fortune. To the Chinese, the dragon represents wisdom, power and dignity, qualities to which Maxxis and Kian Hon wholeheartedly aspire. So the dance was fitting.

Finally, it was time for us to head for the makeshift stage to give our speeches. The beating of kompang (traditional Malay drum) accompanied our passage along the aisle, flanked by guests seated on both sides. When we reached the stage, a group of Chinese drummers positioned there picked up from the kompang beats to extend a boisterous welcome.

I spoke about Kian Hon and Maxxis' commitment to sustainability and maximum efficiency, and our support for the construction of new retreading plants in Indonesia and the Philippines, projected for completion in 2013. Yang Nam spoke about producing the best-quality tread rubber and the safest retread tyres in Southeast Asia. He also spoke of the growth Kian Hon had achieved, at the rate of 10 per cent a year. In 2010, its business turnover was US$50 million, but with the opening of the new facility, he expected it to increase by 2013 to US$65 million.

To express our hopes for the future, we ended the ceremony with a final ritual — the release of butterflies. To Asians, this symbolises longevity and prosperity, again fitting for the occasion because these are the goals Maxxis and Kian Hon harbour for their future, separately and together. Like the butterflies, we aim to make the sky our limit and our flight ahead full of possibilities. We were, as always, looking at the long term, but we had made a new start that day. And 12-12-12 seemed like an auspicious date.

FRUGALITY
AND
INNOVATION

FRUGALITY AND INNOVATION

> It is better not to proceed at all than to proceed without purpose.
>
> — Kung Fu-tzu
>
> 盲從不如不從 (孔子)

FRUGALITY AND INNOVATION are vital to any business, whether that business is a multibillion-dollar global corporation or a one-person operation. Nowhere have I seen this truism highlighted more starkly than in a Japanese book called *Gabai Granny*, a true story about a grandmother surviving poverty after WWII. It was a dark period, in which an economic downturn preceded a prolonged depression. Companies were scaling down. Businesses were closing. To say that times were tough would be an understatement.

Times were even tougher for the old lady who had to raise seven grandchildren by herself. Failing to secure a job, she earned her living by collecting and selling recyclable materials from the streets.

Somehow, she managed to support her grandchildren. Nonetheless, food shortages combined with her meagre income made hunger a daily reality. In desperation, she resorted to collecting rotten fruit and vegetables by the river for food.

As collecting recyclable materials was her best source of income, she came up with an ingenious way to maximise her collection whenever she went out to the streets. She attached a magnet to a string tied around her waist! This one innovative act significantly increased her daily collection of recyclable materials, at almost no cost. A simple magnet allowed this grandmother to overcome her predicament. I continue to be inspired by this story.

THE mRED INITIATIVE

While it isn't the only factor, scarce resources is one of the main reasons organisations practise frugal innovation. We at Maxxis have adopted a strategy which emphasises both frugality and innovation. Maxxis wants to share this strategy, which not coincidentally places a priority on green practices, with our TBR (truck and bus radial) tyre customers.

As we all know, tyres are consumable products which have to be replaced frequently. When they are worn out, the traditional practice has been to dispose of the old tyres and replace with new ones. If this practice continues through the coming decades, how many tyres will be wasted? How many landfills will be created?

To overcome this vicious cycle, we came up with the idea of retreading used tyres using Maxxis' pre-cured rubber compound. We call it "mRED".

I believe that our operation in Malaysia represents an ideal collaboration, whereby Maxxis supplies the rubber masterbatch and our Malaysian distributor, Kian Hon, handles the retreading process. Through this initiative, customers get to retread their old Maxxis TBR tyre casings with Maxxis' rubber compound and tread patterns, and effectively reuse them as new tyres.

This operation is environmentally friendly and the customer saves money — without compromising on tyre quality. It is a winning proposition for everyone involved, which is why mRED stands for **M**aximum **R**esistance, **E**co-friendliness and **D**urability and is marketed under the tagline "Love the Colour, Save the World".

EVERYONE DOES WHAT THEY DO BEST

Being frugal does not mean being cheap. It simply means maximising efficiency by allowing everyone to do that which they do best.

In the case of mRED, Maxxis produces the rubber masterbatch, duplicating the rubber compound used for its new tyres, without a lot of additional time and labour. And Kian Hon uses the mRED pre-cured rubber compound to retread used tyres, just as they have been doing for the past 30 years. We hope to extend the mRED initiative to other interested Maxxis family members through consultation and advice on setting up their own retreading plants.

VALUE FOR MONEY

When costs such as land procurement, equipment and facility investment are removed, the price of a Maxxis retreaded tyre becomes more affordable for customers. The reason is straightforward: Lower start-up costs result in a shorter time needed to achieve positive ROI (return on investment) and thus a lower product price.

A typical retreaded tyre costs as much as 70 per cent less than a new TBR tyre. I believe that this lower tyre cost will attract new customer

segments and create new needs in the market. This collaboration also ensures that customers receive maximum value for every Maxxis tyre they purchase.

mRED is engineered exactly like a new Maxxis tyre, with the same rubber compound and tread patterns. It is crucial to have Maxxis retreaded tyres tailored according to different weather and road conditions in different countries, because this helps to eliminate variable factors which may affect tyre durability and performance. In short, Maxxis tyres, be they new or retreaded, should be of the highest quality.

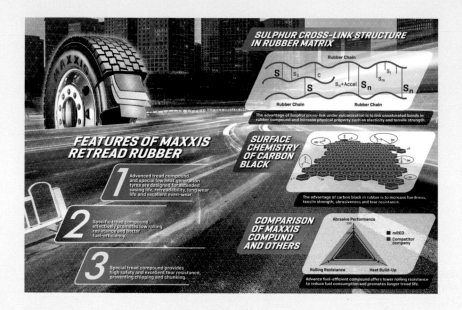

Retreading Boosts Sustainability

For every new TBR tyre which is later retreaded, we can save up to a total of three tyres on the road. Each retreaded tyre uses 70 per cent less oil and raw materials than a new tyre. Maxxis envisions reducing any negative impact on the environment even further and encourages its family members to do the same.

Bring 'It' to Marketing

Frugal marketing is the idea that you don't have to spend a lot of money to be an effective marketer. In fact, you'll often be a better marketer if you spend less, but wisely. By keeping costs down, you'll be profitable sooner!

I believe that deploying new, creative innovations with frugal marketing is imperative. I strongly encourage Maxxis' marketing team to walk the unknown path. I want them to be bold and different.

PEOPLE ARE OUR BIGGEST ASSETS

At the Kuala Lumpur International Auto Saloon Exhibition 2012, the Maxxis 4×4 Club tested this frugal strategy by transforming a bare exhibition space of 3m × 3m with only a modified 4×4 vehicle. The booth had a custom-made 60-degree ramp and two Maxxis Ambassadors in attendance — one who went around making contacts while the other was stationed at the 4×4 vehicle. Our booth was a crowd-puller with the public and media; our team made a lot of new contacts, and our staff smiled for the cameras.

Spending less on booth decorations at a trade show and getting our staff to walk the floor to approach people, instead of spending excessively to decorate the booth in hopes of attracting the crowd, was a smart approach. Booth decorations can be copied, but sincerity and amicability can never be duplicated. People are our most important assets to improve brand image and goodwill; the T3 plus 2 philosophies are constantly translated to Maxxis consumers and eventually to the public *through people*.

Our Maxxis Ambassadors at a photoshoot; (overleaf) tyre performance testing by 4×4 Club members.

UNITING ALL UNDER ONE CORE STRATEGY

UNITING ALL UNDER ONE CORE STRATEGY

> When it is obvious the goals cannot be reached, don't adjust the goals, adjust the action steps.
>
> — Kung Fu-tzu
>
> 射有似乎君子，失諸正鵠，反求諸其身 (孔子)

IT IS MOST IMPORTANT that every stakeholder in an organisation understands the company's core values and strives for a common goal. I believe that this practice helps shape and nurture a strong culture across the company. In 2011, I composed the first *Letter from the President* to stakeholders. I started the letter by analysing the current market outlook and global economy, and then expressed my vision and mission for the company.

In succeeding versions of my annual letter, I have often chosen a specific theme, be it my philosophy for running a business or a strategy I would like to advocate and share, to be included in my letter. I would like to unite shareholders, employees and customers using one core strategy for greater achievement and competitive advantage.

With a new vision to spur us forward each year, I encourage empowerment of employees and customers, promote creative methods for collaboration, and support innovative allocation of resources. I am always surprised and gratified by the new ideas that are brought forward as a result. These ideas are tabled and discussed among our top management to re-evaluate and redefine objectives and strategies for the organisation as a whole.

Sharing goals strengthens an organisation and drives it to a higher level. The responses to my letter are typically positive. For instance, a handful of distributors share insights regarding the tyre industry in their respective countries so as to help us further understand their market on a more nuanced level. Some suggest ways for Maxxis to capitalise on their unique economic situation and thus further improve business strategies to maximise the benefits in sales and publicity. The results are clear, with two-digit growth for Maxxis each year.

SENSE OF URGENCY

The letter also reinforces what I wish to fortify among our stakeholders. I write to ensure that the message is transmitted to everyone. To illustrate this point, I encourage a sense of urgency. A sense of urgency means that you strive to complete an assignment without unnecessary delays. In short, it is to solve a problem in the shortest time possible. I am proud of the fact that across our company, every email from customers gets a response within 24 hours.

In 2012, I decided to reinforce Maxxis' core values through the letter. I urged readers to stay alert and be ahead of the game by having a sense of urgency in their work. Time is of the essence, for time cannot be bought or reclaimed. Procrastination is the cause of failure.

After the letter was circulated, I was very pleased to find that our distributors also practised this value in their business dealings.

A good example of someone who demonstrates this sense of urgency is Shin Yi Tan, who orchestrated the first production of Maxxis coffee. The project was first proposed at a business meeting in Taiwan. She managed to identify a reputable manufacturer, shortlist a few popular flavours, propose and present packaging designs and visuals, and finally deliver the end products in a mere three months!

REFOCUS THE RULES OF THE GAME

The letter was a good start in using direct communication to reshape our corporate culture. Shortly afterwards, a plan was devised to build on this idea. We've long had excellent relationships with our distributors throughout Africa and Asia, where many emerging economies have seen strong growth and steadily rising GDP in recent years. We decided to organise a Maxxis Asian & African Distributor Conference to bring our family members from these two continents together under one roof. The first, in 2012 in Pattaya, Thailand, went very well. By the second year, the conference had grown into a remarkably successful event which we hope to repeat every year.

Held at different locations every year, the conference fosters creativity and innovation, instils a sense of family among the Maxxis participants, and creates and nurtures excellence. It also serves as an additional way to show appreciation to our distributors.

The 2013 Conference: Fostering Creativity

The second conference was held in Penang, Malaysia, a beautiful setting for what turned out to be an inspiring and successful event. As we had done the previous year, we began with presentations by Maxxis representatives from Taiwan, the U.K. and North America, followed by presentations by our distributors from Africa and Asia.

These presentations, especially those by our distributors, served multiple purposes. Communicating with them at the conference, we were able to identify problems and opportunities early, formulate creative initiatives nimbly and implement strategies quickly. Each distributor was given the opportunity to speak to the entire group. There were no restrictions; we welcomed any form of suggestions and comments.

The topics covered in 2013 ranged from warehouse management to cost efficiency, frugal marketing concepts and unique sponsorship collaborations.

Enjoying a city tour to take in the culture of Penang, June 2013.

Dr Wally Chen at the conference.

Of course, providing a safe and encouraging environment is important to ensure that presenters feel motivated to share their best practices. During my talk, I shared my philosophy. I elaborated on the Elevator Theory and the Maxxis Curve — resulting in Value-Up strategies. I explained the theme of the conference and encouraged everyone to be Number One in their territory. I showed my deepest gratitude to all the distributors as well as our suppliers. One of our suppliers, ExxonMobil, was invited to give a presentation explaining how rolling resistance affects cost efficiency in fleets. More importantly, I promised support for a global framework of the Maxxis family by inviting Maxxis USA and Maxxis UK to share their expertise at the conference.

Innovative ideas are often formulated when people feel at ease. Details are important, so nurturing creativity among conference participants started from the moment delegates walked into the ballroom. The atmosphere blew them away. The cosy ambience was enhanced by the right music and soft lighting across the room. To encourage conversation and lessen formality, we had round tables, instead of the side-by-side arrangement common at so many similar events. The proceedings on stage were projected live on both sides of the room so delegates could follow what was going on. Because we knew that they would be sitting for long periods, we asked for bigger tables to provide them with more space and comfort. We steered clear of the classroom and auditorium setting. Drinks and refreshments were served outside the ballroom during breaks. All of our efforts were focused on making delegates feel welcome and comfortable.

During the conference, anticipation was high among the audience for each speaker's presentation. The delegates were eager to listen to and respond to the speakers on the stage. Full respect was given to the speakers, which made it easier for them to give their presentations.

MARKETING INNOVATION

The conference theme, "Rise to New Heights", was incorporated into many of the presentations. Malaysian distributor Kian Hon presented many unusual yet innovative marketing concepts. An arrangement with a local TV producer, for whom the Maxxis 4×4 Club served as a consultant in a travellogue, resulted in valuable free media exposure. The value-to-cost ratio of such an arrangement is high — straight advertising would have been much more expensive.

USE IT TO YOUR BENEFIT — VIA THINKEDGE

The presentation on Maxxis' new network, the ThinkEdge Club, was also well-received. ThinkEdge links customers, employees and principals, gathering and sharing extensive data on what customers want. It allows members to interact and share time-tested ideas on products and strategies, and acts as a Maxxis think tank for R&D and future product development. It also allows Maxxis family members to save time and effort, because they always have someone to consult regarding marketing, sales or human resources.

Through ThinkEdge, Maxxis family members have access to the latest in marketing tools, updated analysis of industry trends and exclusive training materials. Technical know-how on retreading is also available, as is a special task force to help members set up their own retreading plant.

A Look at Retreading

We thought that a tour of Kian Hon's new retreading plant would be interesting and productive for our distributors. We wanted participants to see for themselves what's involved in the retreading process. During the tour, mRED and the retreading process were demonstrated to enhance technical understanding. The tour received enthusiastic response, and many delegates consequently decided that retreading may well be their next venture.

Been There, Done That: The Maxxis Family Experience

A strong sense of family was evident during the awards and cultural nights. Maxxis is a truly global family, creating and nurturing a strong sense of belonging by constantly reinforcing the Triple 3 values of respect, care and appreciation. The entire conference, including the evenings dedicated to culture and to the presentation of awards, reflected those values.

On awards night, an enormous carved ice sculpture symbolised our distributors' countless contributions to Maxxis' success. So that they would have a lasting memento of our appreciation, we gave them trophies. We also recognised distributors who had been with us for 10, 15 and 25 years by giving them special awards. Our distributors enjoyed an evening highlighted by delectable food, eclectic ballroom decorations, first-class performances and wonderful live music.

(top) Kian Hon's new building in Penang; (above) taking a tour
at Kian Hon's new retreading plant.

Maxxis International, in collaboration with Kian Hon Tyres Sdn. Bhd., launches mRED, a premium TBR tread liner providing a total cost solution to Maxxis TBR customers during the 2013 Asian & African Distributor Conference in Penang.

The students of Dalat International School.

Cultural night was also immensely successful. Adventurous guests gathered to try out some local activities, such as blowpipe blowing and dancing with bamboo poles. Guests mingled outside the dining room, reluctant to break off conversations even for dinner.

The cultural dances and instrumental music performances were specifically chosen to welcome delegates from different regions, and these received the most attention during the night. The performances were interactive and the audience were invited to sing and dance along. For example, our Indian delegates were thrilled when Indian dances were introduced on stage and they happily joined in.

MAXXIS MAKES A DIFFERENCE

As I've noted earlier, the importance of giving is a key aspect of Maxxis' shared values. It was important to all of us at Maxxis that some portion of the conference should be devoted to helping those less fortunate. We found an opportunity to contribute to the community around our Maxxis training facility in Penang at the Dalat International School.

One way this school teaches students the value of giving to others is through their sports programme. Dalat participates in a sports tournament that incorporates community service into competition. Eight schools from Malaysia, Thailand, Taiwan, Philippines, Hong Kong, Japan and Guam travel to a tournament for six sports each year, hosted by one of the schools.

What makes these tournaments unique is that the student athletes and coaches spend one day during the tournament to reach out to the local community where the tournament is being hosted. Last year, the girls spent an entire day at an orphanage in the Philippines playing with the kids, teaching them to swim as well as English. The boys brought food to hundreds of families in a poor village.

Together with Kian Hon, we provided team uniforms for the boys' and girls' basketball teams, outfitting them for their state tournament. We also donated tyres for their school vans to ensure that they arrived at all their games safely and on time.

These sports teams also host basketball and soccer camps all over Asia for younger children. During dinner, some of Dalat's student athletes spoke about their experience in countries throughout Southeast Asia serving others when they were off the court and field. We were all moved to hear their stories and delighted to see these young people who have incorporated service to others into their lives.

A sum of US$8000 was raised during the night to support education and service to others. It was a very successful and meaningful fundraising event. I am proud and happy that Maxxis can help make a difference to those in need.

OUR DISTRIBUTORS ARE PART OF THE MAXXIS FAMILY

The night concluded with delegates sharing their feelings about this year's conference. Like everyone there, I was touched to hear what they had to say. Distributors praised the warm hospitality and most of the participants said that they felt the conference had been rewarding, informative and truly amazing.

Along with the other members of Maxxis' management in attendance, I was humbled by the experience of meeting personally with so many members of this wonderful family. It was both an experience I won't forget and one I look forward to repeating every year at this annual gathering.

TO BE
NUMBER
ONE

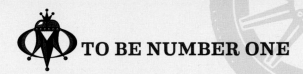# TO BE NUMBER ONE

> You cannot open a book without learning something.
> — Kung Fu-tzu
>
> 開卷有益 (孔子)

AT MAXXIS, WE FEEL almost as though we are in a global contest, competing against all-comers. To be Number One, we have to strive for perfection. I decided we had to go global because Taiwan is a small market and if we stayed there and failed to branch out, we would not be able to survive.

My personal philosophy is that Taiwan as a country is not on par with, say, the U.S. or Japan. In terms of manufacturing, people think of Japan as the best. In education, people think of the U.S. because of its top schools and the number of Nobel Prize winners it has produced. Branding is also Number One in the U.S. and business models that emerge from there always make the news. Europe is known for its profound history and for the fact that a good number of its established companies have been doing business for more than a hundred years.

In the face of all that, how does Taiwan become Number One?

As an entrepreneur, I have to learn from Japan. I have to learn about its manufacturing standards, quality control measures and work ethics. I have to learn from the U.S. — about branding, innovation, creating ideas and marketing. I have to learn from Europe about focusing on the best technology available to me and how to harness technology to achieve durable quality. European cars are a great example of this effective use of technology; they last a long time. European technology is deep and integral to European society.

I learn from the best that all these countries have to offer and the totality resulting from what I learn can help me surpass them. I can never surpass them individually, but, like the results in a school examination, if I add up the marks from each of the several subjects, I might get a total score that can propel me beyond them.

I have an advantage because I'm willing to open myself to absorbing from them. I read Japanese management books in Japanese as well as in translation, and I read Western ones in English. I read a lot because I'm eager to learn, to pick up new ideas. I read three to five management books a month. And I make a lot of notes, on the book itself or in my iPhone. This constant learning process is one way via which anyone can improve.

We are fortunate to be in a strategic position. The Asian region is economically stable. It is going to be the centre of the tyre manufacturing industry. We have the markets. We have competitive labour. We work with our neighbouring countries — they provide the labour, we provide the capital. We also have an advantage in the fact that Taiwan is neutral, which means we can do business in countries like Iran.

The growth in business in emerging markets, like the Middle East, Africa and Asia, has been phenomenal. Emerging markets are actually a key source of our strength as a company, in contrast to more developed nations which are dominated by the giant companies. These established corporate titans are tough for a relatively new competitor to shake. If I were to invest in France, for example, I know before I start that I'm at a disadvantage because French customers prefer Michelin.

THE PRESIDENT AND THE FISH NET

A fishing net is a useful metaphor for another principle: I have to put the net in the right locations so that we can catch more fish. All the departments of the company help to both stretch the net further and keep the fish in. Everyone helps and everyone counts when it comes to building a company and sustaining it.

However, if some part of the net is torn, the fish will escape. My job as the leader is to patch the holes, so I have to be on the lookout all the time. This applies as much to the places we invest in as to the company itself. If any department is not doing well — R&D, marketing, sales, whichever — I need to get it to buck up. I need to concentrate on critical areas to maintain the net's optimal function. Otherwise, our catch will not increase.

The U.S. market is saturated and highly competitive. Although the country is big and you'd expect demand for your products to be high, the intense competition there causes prices to be low. On top of that, you can easily be exposed to litigation. Sometimes, you can be sued in the event of an accident even though it's not the fault of

Dr Wally Chen in New Zealand with Maxxis distributor Tyremax in front of a local dealer's shop.

your tyres. This exposure to the risk of litigation could make us lose our competitiveness.

But on the whole, we don't want to sell a lot of tyres in any one place. In fact, we try not to depend on any single region too much. We have a limited capacity, and so we prefer to sell our tyres where we want. We like selling to customers whom we view as important to us in the long term.

We are always on the lookout for new markets. We have started to make inroads in Cambodia and Myanmar, which are beginning to open up to more foreign investment. The next market we will be looking at in a big way is Indonesia. It is a huge market with huge possibilities.

To keep up with the demand arising from new and emerging markets, we have been building new plants, some simultaneously.

Few companies would build several new manufacturing plants at once because it is inherently risky. But sometimes, you have to take risks.

I believe in testing ideas to see where they take us. When we test a new product in the market, we must do it quickly. A sense of urgency is important. If we fail, we fail earlier, and we fail cheaply. We waste no time in getting back to the drawing board and studying what went wrong. Then we start again, maybe with a different approach, a different strategy. If this time the response is good, we put more investment into it. Our process is one of constant discovery. But the important thing is to try, because we won't know until we try. I'm a curious person; I always want to try.

Don't Say 'Cheese', Say 'Maxxis!'

I learned about branding by trying. There was no one to teach me how to negotiate prices for sponsoring events, how to choose the right vehicle to sponsor, or how to amplify effects from promotion. In Asia, we didn't have big global brands from which to learn when I started. Professors can teach you how to do it by the book, but that's not enough. You have to gain experience for yourself.

And of course, I am constantly increasing our product value by investing in branding and marketing. Every time I make a speech, I include the tagline, "Always branding, always creating value." Some companies assign the responsibility of branding to the marketing department, but at Cheng Shin, I am directly responsible. I read books about branding, study the trends and decide which strategies we should adopt.

I have learned that we need to bring about continuous innovation. We need to keep our products young and dynamic so that people are always talking about them. We need to keep the conversation going.

Don't say cheese, say Maxxis! At the National Yunlin
University of Science and Technology (YunTech),
after I gave a speech there.

And people's tastes change, so we have to keep up with their evolving
preferences to show that we care for their needs. If we cannot produce
new products every year, we can come up with new services and new
merchandise to create fresh topics of discussion, another means of
innovation. We have been developing secondary products which carry
our brand name, like Maxxis Grass Jelly Honey and Maxxis White
Coffee. Although they have nothing to do with tyres, they still add
value to the brand. They also add an element of fun to an otherwise
staid business. We also add a tone of lightheartedness to the simple
activity of taking a group photograph. We ask everyone posing for
the camera to say "Maxxis!" And everyone comes out smiling in the
picture. That's an instance of real-time branding!

Aiming to Be a Love Mark

Of course, we can't be successful with every branding exercise. There are no guarantees. But when we are successful, the benefits we derive can be inexhaustible. That's because brands are exclusive and no one can counterfeit them. But your brand must have substance; it must have a cultural element. If it is established merely through spending a lot of money, your brand will not have lasting power. Harley Davidson is a strong brand because it has strong content. It encapsulates the freestyle, freewheeling American spirit and derives its uniqueness from that. Even the sound of its engine is a trademark. A strong brand must also conjure an experience for the consumer that leaves a lingering impression. Singapore Airlines patents the fragrance of its cabin, an aroma called Stefan Floridan Waters. This fragrance is sprayed on the uniform of the airline's female flight attendants and on all the hot towels given to passengers. People remember the experience of the fragrance long after they have left the plane.

We have based our brand on the promise of quality, service and trust. And we hope that's what people will think of when they see the name Maxxis. Quality is essential because our products are related to safety. While all businesses are about people selling to people, the product variance in our industry is not that big, so service is crucial. As for trust, we instil faith in our distributors so that they know that as long as they meet our requirements, we will not give our business to anyone else. This is good for them as well as for us. They feel they have a free hand to conduct business without having to worry about competition, and we can have an arrangement that is more than just temporary. That helps to establish our trust in them. If distributors are short-term, we would consequently have to incur more trading hours and transaction costs checking on them constantly.

At present, we realise we still have some way to go in developing the status of our brand. It's not enough to be just a trademark, it needs to be a "family mark", something that consumers don't only recognise but also love and respect, like Apple and Starbucks. Some consumers have such an affinity for those brands that if someone criticises Apple or Starbucks, they will speak out to vehemently defend the brand or product.

Sometime in the future, Maxxis may become a platform of multiple brands, which would help to increase our market share. It would be like Sony, which has Walkman radios, Vaio notebooks and Bravia TV sets. As it is, we produce different categories of products, from bicycle tyres to passenger car tyres to truck and bus tyres, which also means we have a broad customer base, ranging from three-year-olds to 80-year-olds. If we can establish a few more brands, the market segmentation might bring us more business. We now offer Bighorn and Razr tyres, which are becoming increasingly popular. People know they are made by Maxxis; and at some point, they might become individual brands.

To increase brand exposure, our sponsorship campaigns continue. People sometimes ask whether sponsorships help to increase tyre sales. I reply that it is difficult to estimate the effects in such an easily quantifiable way; in fact, it is unnecessary to do so. What we want is to reach as high a level of media exposure as we can in order to increase brand awareness among consumers. Besides, our employees feel proud of the company when they see our brand name associated with high-profile sports teams such as the New York Yankees or events such as the Australian Open Tennis Championships.

We sponsor sports extensively because many people follow sports and it is an activity with positive implications. I like sports myself, although my personal liking for it does not influence what we sponsor. When I was a student, I played table tennis, basketball and volleyball. I also played snooker. And because I like to try new things, and because the sport has health benefits, I took up tennis when I was in my fifties. Before that, I was playing golf, but that took too much of my time, sometimes as much as a whole day. I was then working a six-day week so if I played on Sundays, I would have no time for my wife. I hired a coach to teach me tennis and because I have been playing sports all my life, I could pick it up quite easily. I also read books on tennis to help me improve my game. A desire to improve in whatever I do comes naturally to me.

Sports and Sax

Playing sports has helped me in business. Sports helped me to learn about trust and teamwork. From playing doubles in table tennis, I learned how to anticipate the moves my partner would make. I apply that lesson to business. From golf, I learned how to set prices. For example, a whole bag of ten golf clubs might cost $330, and although the price is economical, it might not contain the one excellent driver that can help me hit the ball as far as I'd like. Would I still buy it? What if I find elsewhere a single club that suits my needs, but it costs $1,000? Would I buy that instead? If it will let me hit the ball five yards further, yes, I would be willing to pay the price for it. On that score, if we have a product that is worthy and nothing else can compare, people will pay for it. We can set a higher price and have no problems selling it if the product meets the buyer's requirements. At the same time, we still cater to those who would settle for the lower-priced bag of clubs. We produce a range of tyres with different prices. We have Maxxis tyres that are priced higher than Cheng Shin tyres.

But we still maintain quality for all the tyres we produce, regardless of the price at which they are sold.

Another new thing I've picked up recently is playing the saxophone. At my age, it's not that easy, but I try, because I learn things from music.

In a quest to broaden my intellectual horizons, I opted to study for my Executive Master in Business Administration (EMBA) at the National Jiao Tung University in Hsinchu, realising my long-time dream to do a post-graduate course. I didn't want to go back to my alma mater, National Taiwan University, in Taipei because it would have been too far. Besides, the National Jiao Tung University is a good school. Starting in September 1998, I went there on weekends to attend classes, travelling one-and-a-half hours from Yuanlin. I got the opportunity to make friends and learn from other students. They also learned from me because I came to the classroom with real-life business experience. I'm happy to say that I completed the course in June 2001.

Then in 2012, I felt very honoured to be awarded an honorary doctorate by the National Yunlin University of Science and Technology (YunTech). I gave an acceptance speech in which I talked about the Maxxis Elevator Theory, the Maxxis Curve and Triple 3.

Degrees aside, the more you learn, the less you know. Every year, new management books come out and new ways of doing business are presented. My knowledge is never enough because the world is ever-changing. I fully believe that you are what you read.

FRUGAL AND FRACTAL

I am learning about the fractal business model, which has helped me to understand that as we get bigger, we need to decentralise more. From

Receiving the honorary doctorate from the president of YunTech, Dr Yang Yeong Bin in 2012.

My wife and daughter sharing in my joy at the honorary doctorate presentation.

headquarters, I can only motivate, inspire and provide the necessary support for our overseas branches; I do not get directly involved or tell other operations to do everything that I want in the way that I prefer. If I have to send instructions to our branches all over the world on what to do, delays will result and quick decisions or actions cannot be taken. I motivate and inspire our team with the Triple 3 concept, and I lay the foundation for our company culture, but I leave the rest to them. They take that on board and use it to guide their own decisions. I have to be the role model and follow our guiding principles. Our team members take their cue from me.

I am learning frugal engineering from India, where they can produce the Tata Nano, a car that is sold at US$2,200, the cheapest in the world, or the Godrej portable refrigerator that runs on a battery and is sold at US$60. The quality need not be inferior; it is simply a case of achieving more with fewer resources and cutting down on non-essential features. In India, they can design virtually anything at a low cost. I think this is a future trend. We are facing a scarcity of resources. We may run out of water long before we run out of oil. We should be looking at using frugal engineering to lower our tyre production costs.

Our collaboration with Kian Hon, our distributor in Malaysia, to start a training centre there and to also expand Kian Hon's retread production line is based on the frugal business model. Cheng Shin did not spend any money setting up this centre, but we can ask our distributors from all over Asia and elsewhere to visit for knowledge exchange and learn about the retreading process from Kian Hon. For the retread business, Cheng Shin makes money by providing Kian Hon the mixed rubber. Kian Hon produces the tread liners and teaches others how to do retreading. Kian Hon makes money too, so everybody wins. In such a situation, some other giant company might want to take over 51 per cent of Kian Hon, but we don't need to. We follow not only the frugal way, but the fractal way as well.

I am learning that as a leader, it's important that I must be humble and not arrogant. I must practise self-reflection, maintain a balanced viewpoint, listen to all sides, look from all perspectives and have self-confidence. Confucius said one must practise self-reflection three times a day. That is sound advice.

THE WORLD IS MY STAGE

I learned from reading the book *Living in More than One World* by Bruce Rosenstein that it's not enough to just go to work every day. You need to ask yourself how your work benefits other people. You

"The world is my stage."

need to have outside interests, or you will find it hard to mature as a person. You need to gain self-knowledge and consciously work to develop new skills. In short, you need to live a multi-dimensional life in order to develop as a total human being. Recently, our Nigerian distributor gave me a piece of calligraphy which reads, "The world is my stage." (世界我舞台). It is. And I like that very much.

The world is also Maxxis' stage. And all the men and women in it play a part in making it a success. Our industry is, after all, a people-centred one. When we have a problem, we try to solve it by asking who caused it, what method was applied, which material was used and which machine processed it. But if you analyse each of the elements involved, you will find that every problem has its roots in people. Methods and machines are designed by people, and as for the material, someone procured it.

I put up a sign in our office that says, "Be sure to bring your head with you every day." Without brains, we cannot compete with other companies and other countries. I tell my staff that if things don't go well, we should not attribute it to external factors, but to ourselves.

Maxxis must also keep its focus. We don't diversify. We stick to what we are doing in order to do it well. We aim high, far and wide. We look at the long term. We look at lifetime relationships, not short-term gain. We are here to stay, together as a family. I want Maxxis to be a human-based, culture-rich company. I want Maxxis to be a dynasty.